Your dark side

How to turn your inner negativity into positive energy

VIVIANNE & CHRISTOPHER CROWLEY

Thorsons

Thorsons
An Imprint of HarperCollins*Publishers*
77–85 Fulham Palace Road
Hammersmith, London w6 8jb

The Thorsons website address is: www.thorsons.com

Published by Thorsons 2001

1 3 5 7 9 10 8 6 4 2

A catalogue record for this book
is available from the British Library

ISBN 0 7225 3877 4

Printed and bound in Great Britain by
Martins the Printers Limited, Berwick upon Tweed

Contents

Acknowledgments

There are always many people to thank in a book such as this, which is drawn on personal and sometimes painful experiences. The people you read about here are real people, but unless they are in the public eye, we have changed their names and crucial identifying features of their lives. In addition to those who must remain anonymous, we would like to thank Jean, Jim, Clare and Paul who helped us devise the Dark Side Quiz, and Carole Tonkinson, our editor, who first thought of this project.

Other shadow workers who have helped us on our journey – Debbie Ford inspired the word exercise in Chapter 7 and Ellie Baker's shamanic journey inspired us to use cave imagery to help elicit the shadow. Liz McCormick's training in brief therapy showed us ways of helping people examine their life history. A 1970s survey by the magazine *Psychology Today* gave us the idea for the money worries quiz in Chapter 8. The work that gave rise to this book began with our training in transpersonal therapy. We remain grateful always to the Centre for Transpersonal Psychology in Britain for the training we received with the late Ian Gordon-Brown, and with Barbara Somers, Joan and Reyn Swallow, and Liz McCormick, who first introduced us to our own shadows and to many of the therapeutic techniques and exercises we use in our work.

1)

What is your
dark side?

*The only devils in the world are those
running around in our hearts.
That is where the battle should be fought.*

Mahatma Gandhi, Indian nationalist
leader and spiritual guru.

Are you the person you would like to be? Are you even the person you pretend to be? If you were honest, you would have to reply, 'No.' Each of us has a public face, a way of presenting ourselves to the world. This is a cleaned-up version. It is what we want others to see. To a certain extent, this is essential if we are to live in a civilized society. We have to fit in and co-operate with others. This *persona* or *whitewashed self* is part of you, but it is not the 'real' you. We have another side, a private side that is not for public view. In the darkened backrooms of the psyche lurk the secret fears and fantasies that lie beneath our surface personalities.

What happens to these hidden feelings and emotions? Repressed in the deepest and ignored parts of our psyches, they do not wither away. They grow more powerful in the darkness until, volcano-like and triggered by sometimes trivial causes, they explode their way to the surface. Have you ever done something totally out of character? Did you get drunk at the office party, seduce your best friend's boyfriend, or sabotage a promising relationship by suddenly venting a tirade of jealousy and anger? Did a side of you leak out that you wanted to keep hidden? Did you let someone see another aspect of your personality – and it wasn't a pretty sight? This is the dark side that we all possess but would rather forget.

We suppress in the unconscious all kinds of negative thoughts and feelings that we do not want even our partners or best friends to know about. This doesn't mean that everything in the unconscious is negative. The unconscious is an unexplored country. There are mountains and plains, valley and viewpoints, swamps and flower-filled fields. There are dark caves and resources waiting to be tapped. What will we find there? It may be a brave and heroic side of us that emerges only in extreme conditions. It may be a fearful child who must be cared for and helped to grow. It may be a fearsome wild beast, a dangerous snake, or a mythical beast with the power of healing. All these are hidden parts of us. Our lives will have developed so that these parts of our psyches have been neglected, forgotten or we may not know them as ours, but they exist. Deep in our unconscious, waiting for their moment, they lie dormant waiting for our call. This is our *potential* or *unknown self.*

This book is a journey into the dark side. The dark side is our inner negativity. It includes both what we know about ourselves and what we do not. The pioneering psychiatrist Dr Carl Jung gave the name *shadow* to the part of ourselves we hide from. Potential self contains shadow. It also contains the hidden potential of the *true self* – we as we are meant to be. This book looks at the dark side, the negative aspects of ourselves, both known and unknown, and recognizes the complex and sometimes apparently conflicting web of emotions it contains. The dark side is a multifaceted black diamond buried deep within us – and diamonds are a valuable commodity. This book explores how to access your dark side and how to find that diamond, but it is not a book for people who want instant wonder cures. Instead, we take a sane and realistic view of how we can access our full potential and work through the inner negativity that holds us back.

There are many ways of looking at our dark side. We could see it as a moral problem – as religions do. We could see it as a psychological problem – as psychotherapists do. We prefer to see it more pragmatically. This is a book for independent-minded people who enjoy improving the way they do things. If you like to learn, this book is for you. If your life functions as well as that of the average person – some days things go well, other days things are a bit of a mess – but you would like your life to function a whole lot better, this book is for you. It will help you to live your life more fully and to enjoy being you a whole lot more. As Carl Jung said, 'Realizing the shadow is a practical problem...' We cannot see something clearly when it lurks in the shadows. We trip over it. It gets in the way of where we are going, and where we want to go is forward. Shadow gets in the way of getting the most out of life. Shadow creates obstacles and convoluted thinking and emotions that we do not need. As you learn to spot your shadow's tricks, life becomes simpler, the road straightens out. You can see more clearly where you are heading and where you want to go. You can start being the real you.

⇌

CHANGE

'How many therapists does it take to change a light bulb?'
'Only one, but the light bulb has to really want to change.'

OK, it's an old joke – but it's true. Most people read self-help books because there is something in their lives they would like to change. They would like their lives to work just that bit better. Some of this book is informative: it tells you about your dark side. However, there is little point in learning about your dark side if you do not want to do anything about it, if you do not want to change. This book will help you make the changes you want in your life.

Change is an interesting word. Sometimes we want to change and sometimes we don't. Sometimes we find it difficult to change behaviors and attitudes that are seriously dysfunctional. They are old well-worn riverbeds and when the mountain snows melt, water takes the path of least resistance and cascades down them. Habits of thinking, feeling, speaking and doing are like this. Making changes can require enormous effort. However, change is possible. A Zen teacher once described to us how, when his order moved into their new temple – a 19th-century house in a large city – all the brass door knobs were tarnished. The monks set to work and soon all the inside doors had shining doorknobs. The front door was an exception. The doorknob had not been polished for over a hundred years. The Zen teacher decided to persist. Every Saturday morning for months, he polished the doorknob. For months, nothing happened.

Then, suddenly one morning he saw a tiny golden speck in the tarnish. He had broken through. After this, things progressed quickly. Once the first chink in the tarnish had been made, the rest was relatively easy – but it had taken a long time to get there. Changing ourselves can be rather like this. If we just keep applying a small amount of effort and we do not give in, then eventually the inertia gives way. We change.

⌇⌇

SHADOW SPOTTING

At the end of each chapter, you will find suggestions for things you can do to help you explore your dark side and your potential self. You will find the unconscious patterns and driving forces that lead your life down side turnings, instead of down the highway to being what you want to be. These suggestions are to help you get your life into the right lane – the lane that leads to the true you.

Many of the suggested exercises involve creative work. Maybe you think you are not a creative person, but we all have inner creativity. The human species is one of extraordinary inventiveness. We can all imagine, fantasize, write, draw and paint. Our species can devise solutions to novel problems – anything from thinking of a good marketing strategy, to persuading a child to do something she or he does not want to do, to arranging the furniture in a room, or creating a new software package. We can recognize that a work colleague has good dress sense, see that a painting by a famous artist is beautiful, or be moved by the passionate beauty of a piece of music. We can access our own creativity and recognize creativity in others. We use creativity all the time. The creative exercises are to help you understand your dark side. The processes involved are as helpful as the end product. They will open up your imagination, and imagination can transform our lives.

We ask you to reflect on your present, past and future. Sometimes we ask you to think about your childhood. For some of us childhood is easy to recall, for others so much time has elapsed that childhood seems a distant country, but recognizing the patterns that are laid down in childhood is important. Sometimes we ask you to visualize and use imagery. The power of imagery is widely underestimated, even though visualization is used by everyone from top football teams to solo athletes, to dancers, singers and people suffering from life-threatening diseases. The idea that you can find out about your inner world through visualization exercises may seem unlikely until you try it, but they work.

With most exercises, we suggest that you write down or record the results in some other way, such as drawing. We suggest that you keep all the material that comes to you from the exercises, so that when you reach the end of this book, you can look back upon the work as a whole to see what insights you have gained.

And now to begin: before going on to the next section of the book, try doing a simple exercise to help you explore what you might need to re-evaluate about your life.

GETTING TO KNOW YOUR DARK SIDE

Find a quiet moment when you can be alone, undisturbed by others.

1 Take a sheet of paper and divide it into three columns.

2 At the top of column one write: 'MY DARK SIDE: What I know about myself.' Write down all the negative characteristics of your personality that you can think of. Ignore traits that other people may think of as negative – such as being careful with money – but which you see as sensible thrift. List only those qualities that seem negative to you.

3 Head column two: 'MY DARK SIDE: What others say about me.' Think of someone, preferably of the same sex, who does not like you. Write down the negative qualities this person might say you have. (This doesn't mean, of course, that he or she would be right.) To help, think about things that people have accused you of in the past.

4 Head column three: 'DARK SIDE IN OTHERS: What I dislike in other people.' Think of two or three people whom you most dislike. Write down a list of their negative qualities.

5 Now compare the three columns. Do they share any common characteristics? Are there any commonalities between how a critic might describe you and your description of people you dislike? If so, you will need to work on these areas.

In looking at your negative qualities and writing them down, you are making an admission to yourself. This exercise will not enable us to recognize all our negative patterns; but it is a beginning. Keep your list somewhere safe so you can look at it later.

☆

FIVE THINGS TO REMEMBER:

1 The dark side of ourselves leaps out when we least expect it.

2 Not acknowledging the dark side of ourselves causes us problems. It stops us being the people we want to be.

3 Changing our relationship with our dark side is a creative act – and we are a very creative species.

4 Change can be scary, but a part of us enjoys doing slightly scary things. People go on theme park rides, watch horror movies, drive fast and surf for thrills and fun.

5 You cannot change the past, but the future is yours for the taking.

2

The dark side
and you

*Without the darkness of the night, if all were
bathed forever in the limitless light of the sun,
how would we ever see the stars?*

Dealing with our shadow is as difficult as stepping on it when we
were kids in the schoolyard. Just when we think we've got it – it slips
away from us again. Like a kitten chasing its own tail, we can just
about see it from the corner of our eye, but it keeps on eluding us.

What makes us less than perfect? What makes us less good than
we would like to be? What is it that subverts our good intentions
and makes us act negatively? What makes us less successful than we
know we could be and should be? Our conscious minds are often
painfully aware of our negativity, but powerless to control it. Most
of us aspire to be good, kind, thoughtful and considerate. We try to
'do as we would be done by', to treat others as we hope to be treated
ourselves. We want to act as positively as we can and to be as

successful as we can. Sometimes, however, despite all our best intentions, things go awry. Something bursts out from deep within that wrecks the moment, destroying the mood or the understanding that was building up. The destructive comment, the snide remark, the joke that was meant to be funny but comes across as cruel – it is as if a darker version of us slips its leash. Dark side is out and running free.

To take another example: do you ever find yourself in a situation where you are too ready to defer to others, too ready to put yourself down? Do you find you are denigrating yourself, or not seizing an opportunity that is up for grabs? Do you apologize for things that need no apology, and are not your fault? Do you always aim for second best, setting your targets too low because somehow you cannot believe that good things can happen to you, or that you can ever get exactly what you want? Maybe there is an insistent voice inside you telling you that you are not good enough, not worthy enough to go for what you want? An inner negative force holds you back. The shadow restricts and confines, limiting your potential. It wants to keep you in the dark.

Is there a side of you that you know about, but hide away in shame? It may be sexual, an addiction, or some kind of compulsive behavior, such as an eating disorder – bulimia or anorexia nervosa? It may be latent frustration and anger that burst out only when you get behind the wheel of a car and a minor incident triggers road rage. It may be a gnawing suspicion that makes you sneak looks at your partner's e-mails or rummage through your partner's pockets or purse to check for any evidence he or she is cheating on you. What makes you like this? What creates the neediness? The cause, and the solution, may be hidden deep in your dark side.

EGO

From the moment we are born to our very last breath, we receive messages from other people – that is good, this is bad, I approve or disapprove of what you are doing. From, 'Well done! That's the way to do it!' to, 'Don't ever do that again', we are bombarded continuously with information about how we should behave. Sometimes the messages are overt: 'Stop that at once!' Sometimes it is more subtle: 'Wouldn't it be better if...?' or, 'That's not very nice, is it?' Often messages are subliminal, conveyed in a look or a gesture that speaks far more eloquently and powerfully than any clumsy words.

We learn from this. We could not function in our complex and sophisticated world without this instruction. It helps form our personality, our *ego*. Ego is what we think we are, the conscious self. It combines how we are naturally with learned behavior from childhood. The ego includes all the hopes, fears, memories, achievements and failings that go toward forming our personality. Unfortunately, what we think we are is only part of the truth. Much of the time we are wrong. In the *Tibetan Book of Living and Dying*, Tibetan teacher Sogyal Rinpoche writes that the ego is a false and incorrectly assumed identity. We do not know what we really are and rather than face the whole of ourselves – good and bad – we prefer to hold on to the illusion.

≷≷

PERSONA

As children, we soon find that some behaviors are more acceptable than others. Present this face, display this behavior, do things this way and you will get recognition, praise and reward. These tricks may not be the 'real' you, but they work. In this way our *persona* develops. We are not only what we think we are, the *ego*, we also have a face that we choose to present to the world – the *persona*. Persona is the opposite of your dark side: it is *your whitewashed side*. We are all aware of having an image to maintain, the cleaned up image we present to others. This is not negative. Our personas help facilitate social interaction. In everyday life, at work, on a first date, at the parents group, in our local neighborhood association, we want to interact with others smoothly and easily. We cover our negative characteristics under a veneer of polite pleasantries. If we didn't, society would not function well. Persona is our 'coping with the world' face. Like the movie star's and politician's PR spin, persona is how we wish to appear. Most of us find it a strain to live up to our personas all the time, and most of us do not try. At home in the privacy of family and friends, we 'let it all hang out'. We become our 'normal' selves.

≷≷

NEGATIVE EGO

I'm her and she's me and we're each other.

Mae West on her film character the 'baddie' Diamond Lil in
Goodness had Nothing to do with it.

If *persona* is what we try to show, then *negative ego* is what we try to keep in the closet. *Negative ego* is the dark side that we know about, aspects of ourselves we are ashamed of and want to hide. This starts in childhood – and children's closets are rather small. By the time we reach adulthood, our closets are bursting. Occasionally the door flies open and things tumble out into view – usually when we are trying to impress someone. Embarrassed, we shove the offending items back inside – and turn the key. Dark side is held in – for the time being.

SHADOW

For now we see through a glass, darkly; but then face to face:
now I know in part; but then shall I know even as also I am known.

Holy Bible: 1 Corinthians 13.12 (King James Version)

We know about negative aspects of our personalities – *negative ego*, but there are also negative aspects of ourselves that we do not recognize at all. Much of our negative behavior is unconscious – we are not aware that we are doing it. Carl Jung popularized the term *shadow* for this unconscious negative side of our personalities. The shadow is part of us, but we find it difficult to admit it. The shadow is that which we do not want to be. It is pain, anger, desire for vengeance, jealousy – all our meanest emotions. It is our alter ego, dark twin and inner demon.

The shadow often appears in fiction. The most well known example is Robert Louis Stevenson's *The Strange Tale of Doctor Jekyll and Mister Hyde*. The virtuous doctor is a pillar of respectability in his Scottish Calvinist community. Ostensibly, he is undertaking scientific research, but experimentation with drugs leads him to access his shadow, Mr Hyde. Once accessed, Mr Hyde's power grows as it is not confronted but feared and repressed. It grows through feeding on the fear it creates. As Jekyll's shadow grows, so he has to try ever harder to preserve his normal persona, to 'keep up appearances.' The story was written and set in Victorian times when 'gentlemen' were required to adhere to an exceptionally demanding and rigid social and behavioral code. The unfortunate Dr Jekyll finds his persona ever more impossible to maintain. Hyde grows ever more powerful and, in the battle between the two, both Jekyll and Hyde are destroyed.

⩫

BLIND SPOTS

All of us (well most of us) are aware of some of our negative qualities. We do come across people who think they are perfect, but mercifully they are rare. Why do we instinctively dislike people who believe implicitly in their virtue? Is it because we sense that behind the smooth exterior is a seething cauldron of negative qualities that the individual refuses to acknowledge? People who admit their own imperfections are much easier to like than those who do not. Most of us like to live up to our own self-image. This is normal. The problem is that we often have impulses that displease our egos very much.

They do not match the image we have of ourselves (the ego) or of that which we wish to project (the persona). To maintain our own image of ourselves as good people, the shadow manipulates us into some very convoluted thinking. This is the syndrome of the mother whose jealousy of her pretty daughter leads her always to buy her unattractive clothes so that 'she does not get too full of herself.' It is the father who sends his artistic son to military college, 'because it will be good to toughen him up.' Really, he is afraid that his friends at work may think his son is effeminate and, by extension, that perhaps he is too.

PROJECTION

Projections change the world into the
replica of one's unknown face.

Carl Jung

We not only disguise our own motives, we also project them onto others. Repressed qualities and energy must go somewhere. If we are not prepared to own up to our negative impulses then we will tend to see them in others. How often have you met the miser who talks constantly about how stingy other people are? How often have you come across garrulous bores who pontificate about loudmouths? When we refuse to see our worst faults in ourselves, then we see them in other people. Have you ever heard someone frothing at the mouth about how intolerant people are?

The shadow operates in a peculiar way. It is often at work when we meet people for the first time and take an immediate dislike to them.

I do not like thee, Dr Fell,
the reason why, I cannot tell;
but this I know, I know full well:
I do not like thee, Dr Fell.

Tom Brown, 17th-century writer. Based on the Roman writer Martial

It might just be that they are unpleasant people. However, if you find you intensely dislike someone whom everyone else is convinced is nice, you might be seeing your shadow. If, even worse, this person reminds other people of you, then you almost certainly are seeing your shadow. If we are unaware we possess qualities that we dislike, we project them onto other individuals and social groups. These people then embody all the immature, evil and other repressed tendencies hidden in our shadows. This is an important factor in racial prejudice. When we project our negative qualities onto others, we live in a dangerous world, because it is an illusionary one. We see things in others that are not there – negative things – and this makes us angry.

We know we are projecting aspects of our own psyche when we overreact to what other people say and do. A classic example is the macho redneck who rants endlessly about 'faggots.' The best time of his life was when he was in the army. His only close emotional relationships have been with other men. He loves watching male contact sports like wrestling and boxing. We might ask ourselves whether the aggression masks a secret fear. Chris Cooper portrayed this beautifully in his role as Marine Colonel Fitts in the 1999 Sam Mendes movie *American Beauty.* If your reaction to someone is over the top, do not forget the old saying, 'It takes one to know one.'

Now why, in my teenage years, was I so convinced that all my friends were self-centred and egotistical...?

The shadow contains aspects of ourselves that we dislike, but nothing is wholly good or wholly bad. Many qualities that we learn to repress can be useful if properly channeled. The positive side of anger is energy. The positive side of jealousy can be the impetus we need to do something to improve the quality of our lives. The shadow can be thought of as an energy blockage. Instead of finding a useful way of transforming aspects of situations or ourselves that we do not like, our negative feelings are suppressed and eat away at us. First, we must begin to own the shadow. We must recognize it. Then we learn to accept that part of us. Once this is achieved, we can befriend it. Through this, we can transform it and harness its energy to more positive ends. We can *Recognize, Accept and Befriend* these energies and thus transform them.

⧖ Something to try ⧖
LETTING IN SOME LIGHT

A contrasting image to shadow is that of sunlight. This is an exercise to imagine how it might be to let light enter a little more into your private world. It is often easier to change the externals of our lives than the internals, so why not start with the externals? In Western life today, possessions proliferate and accumulate, but owning too many things is a burden. Our ancestors knew exactly what they owned. Do you? Do you want to possess things that you can't remember owning? If you made a list of how many items you own down to the last fork, pair of socks and CD, how many would it be: one thousand, two, three? If we want to have certain internal conditions in our psyche, it is a good idea to replicate what we want in the external world. If you want your psyche to be focused, uncluttered and easy to access, you need to make your environment focused, uncluttered and easy to access. If you want to know yourself, getting on top of your outer environment is a good place to start.

1   Imagine being bathed in sunlight. Sunlight streams into your room and into every room in your house.

2   You open all the cupboard doors and sunlight streams into these as well. There are no dark corners – everything is on view.

3   How would this work for you really? Would you be able to open up your house and display all your possessions without shame? Most people have piles of junk shoved into lofts, basements, cupboards under stairs, in garages, outbuildings and garden sheds. How would you feel if all your possessions were on show?

4   Supposing that except for clothing with special memories – a wedding dress, a suit you wore for your graduation – you gave away or threw out all the clothes that you had not worn for a year? Would there be a gaping hole in your life, or would deciding what to wear be simpler? Would you be able to see what you owned?

5   To get a handle on your shadow, start getting a handle on your possessions. Investigate the dark and dusty cupboards and see what is there. Then get rid of what you do not need.

6   Many people find it difficult to throw things away, but much easier to give things away. Go through all your possessions –

clothes, books, CDs, household items, and decide what you use and what you do not.

7 If things are broken, then get them mended or throw them out. Often we keep items that seem too expensive to repair, but too good to throw away. All this useless clutter in our lives absorbs our energy in subtle ways. It makes it more difficult to store the items we do want. It creates housework because we need to tidy and dust the possessions we neither need nor want. It is much simpler not to own them at all.

8 Tidy up cupboards. Throw away or give away any items you no longer need. Go through your purse and throw away old supermarket receipts. Tidy up your books, videos, computer discs and CDs.

9 What about your kitchen? Are its cupboards full of old packages of food that you never quite got around to finishing? If so, get rid of them.

10 Now look around your home and open all your cupboards. How do you feel now you are more on top of your environment?

☆

FIVE THINGS TO REMEMBER

1 Your dark side feeds on emotions, hidden fears and unexpressed anger. It inhibits your energy and potential.

2 The more you deal with life by living through a persona, the more you feed the dark side.

3 Try changing small aspects of your environment and see what the knock-on effects might be.

4 Remember that the best way to make lasting changes is to make small gradual changes. Too great or sudden changes, such as overnight transformations, are too much strain. It's like stretching out a piece of elastic. Sooner or later (usually sooner) it snaps back to its original position.

5 Try being more true to yourself in small ways and see what happens. Experiment and enjoy the experience.

3)
The dark side
in childhood

Yesterday upon the stair
I saw a man who wasn't there
He wasn't there again today
Oh how I wish he'd go away.

Traditional nursery rhyme

Shadow represents the things we do not like to talk about, the parts of us we don't acknowledge, the sources of secret shame. But are these parts of us necessarily bad? Some personality characteristics are almost always undesirable. They are instinctual reactions deemed inappropriate in a modern civilized society. Some were acceptable earlier in our lives but not now. These are our selfish responses; the 'Gimme!' of childhood, the unwanted intrusion into another person's possessions, person or space; the 'Me! Me! Me!' syndrome. These stem from reflexes of childhood, even of babyhood, when all we are is a blob of stimuli and receptors biologically geared to only one thing – our need to survive.

As toddlers, we learn about spaces and boundaries. We begin to explore the world around us. Our interactions with others give us a sense of self. We learn to refer to ourselves as '*I*'. Everything that is not *I* is *Other*. *Other* is something to be explored. It is to be prodded and poked, taken and played with, and discarded when a new distraction catches the eye. Take away the object of interest too soon, whether it is a person or thing, and tantrums follow. At this stage, we have little understanding of the independent nature of the Other. It is classic existentialism. The Other exists only while it occupies our short attention spans. It exists only while it remains in our vision. That it may have feelings, that it can feel pleasure or pain, that it has its own will or mind does not come into the equation. Children will cheerfully pull the wings off insects to see what happens. They lack the empathy to know that this is cruel.

At a slightly later age, we begin to learn about our bodies and about the bodies of others, especially those of the opposite sex. We may play doctors and nurses, or other exploratory games. A new awareness of otherness comes into being. Moving on to teenage years, those times of self-consciousness and angst, we define our relationship with the Other in terms of tribal identity. We are trying to discover where we fit in the world. Seeing things in black and white, teenagers are likely to have a small, close-knit circle of friends. Other people do not count, are beyond contempt, or are perceived as actively hostile. The 'enemy' group can include anyone not in our age or peer group – parents, relations, teachers, social workers. Anyone of the same age but not in our clan, which can be differentiated by class, ethnicity, fashion, musical tastes, subjects taken in school – by almost anything – may also be put in this category.

Then we find the 'Other' in another person. We fall in love for the first time. We idolize and idealize that person. We project onto our beloved an image of perfection that no one could ever be or sustain. And our love is different from anything anyone in the whole course of human existence has ever experienced before.

These are snapshots of distinct phases in our lives, but they are phases we are expected to grow through and beyond. We learn from them and move beyond them as unconscious 'rites of passage' take us step-by-step along the road to adulthood. As we progress, we develop new behaviors appropriate to our new circumstances. The old ways of behaving are cast aside. As Saint Paul wrote:

> *When I was a child,*
> *I spoke as a child,*
> *I understood as a child,*
> *I thought as a child:*
> *but when I became a man,*
> *I put away childish things.*
>
> 1 Corinthians 13:11

Putting away childish things is healthy. What happens if we become stuck in outmoded behavior? Perhaps dysfunctional family circumstances meant that we could not work through these stages at the appropriate time. Maybe overbearing or over strict parenting led to their suppression. These repressed behavioral traits, emotions, feelings and learning patterns are the substance of the dark side. The outmoded behaviors still work to some extent so we are reluctant to discard them, but we sense they are not entirely acceptable in the stage of life we are in. We attempt to conceal them, until overpowering self-interest brings them to the surface.

⇌

SEEING DARKNESS CLEARLY

If it is easier to see other people's dark sides than our own, how do we access our dark side? Firstly, we have to want to. We need to recognize and acknowledge the forces that build up inside us. Recognizing and acknowledging the dark side does not mean suppressing or destroying it. To try to suppress these forces would exacerbate and accelerate the crisis. It is like the red hot magma of a volcano surging and seething deep underground waiting for the pressure to build to intolerable levels to eventually violently erupt, showering all around with red hot ash and molten rock and lava flows. If there is an outlet for the pressure, then the crisis need not come to a head. We provide the outlet when we accept that we are far from perfect and we want to do something about it. Only then can we deal with it. Through dealing with it, it becomes less of a problem.

When do we recognize the dark side at work? Often it is when our response to a situation is over the top, a disproportionate reaction to something relatively trivial.

Chris' dark side

I used to become furious if, in conversation, someone didn't hear me properly and I was asked to repeat what I had said. This seemed an intolerable imposition. The volcano erupted and I used to repeat what I had said in an angry shout. Why should it have mattered so much?

I often have to ask people to repeat themselves. I would probably be amazed, angry and hurt if my request met with so much vehemence, so much anger.

Thinking through why I had this disproportionate reaction, I realized it was a defensive reaction masking a fear of being rubbished or mocked. I looked back into my childhood. I was the younger of two sons in a stable and secure family. The only family rows were father and elder brother's discussions about science and politics. My intellectual brother seemed impelled to take the opposite viewpoint to my father in everything. What were supposed to be rational discussions often descended into arguments that I hated. At the time, I had no real interest in these subjects and, being younger, I could not join in at their level. Of course, hating to be ignored, I used to try. Butting in on their train of thought usually meant that I was asked to repeat myself only for my rather feeble contribution to be mockingly dismissed. The resentment I felt at this treatment was stored in my dark side, where it fed and grew. In adulthood, when my unconscious recognized the sequence re-occurring, trapped dark side anger erupted.

Look at your own behavior. Do you ever overreact? Is there a pattern to this overreaction? Do you treat people in a way that you would resent deeply if you were on the receiving end? Answer yes to any of these and you may be recognizing part of your dark side. Most people aspire to 'do as you would be done by'. If there is a disparity between your behavior and what you want from others, the cause may be lying hidden in your shadow self.

SHADOW INFERIORITY

Babies are not born with shadow. It is something that we acquire as we discover that some behaviors and attitudes are acceptable and that others are not. Some aspects of our personalities are acceptable; others are not. Parents, siblings, friends, teachers, religious organizations, the social and political climate in which we live, all these individuals and institutions impinge on us. They teach us there are some aspects of ourselves that must be hidden away. Some of these hidden aspects we know. It is as though we put them away in closets to which we have keys. Other aspects are stored in the basement of the house of the personality. They are hidden amongst the accumulated junk of a lifetime so we may forget we own them at all. We may forget them but they will not have forgotten us. These neglected aspects of our being belong to our childhood selves. Like all normal children, they want to be noticed. Like the things buried in the cellars of horror movies, at night when the conscious mind is sleeping, they try to get out. Shadow stuff emerges in our dreams.

We try to hide certain aspects of ourselves because we are ashamed of them. We do not want other people to look down on us, so we try to pretend to be better than we are. As babies, we are too 'me focused' to think of comparing ourselves with others. As we emerge out of the cocoon of the baby world, doubts set in. Maybe we are not quite as great as we thought. The first flush of enthusiasm of our doting parents may have worn off a bit as well, as the reality of teething and nappies takes its toll. Many people struggle all their lives with secret feelings of inferiority. Tragically, many of those who feel inwardly unsuccessful, and are successful by anyone else's standards, spend their lives convinced that they have got where they are by mistake. Someday someone will find them out and their inferiority and incompetence will be exposed.

Psychiatrist Dr Alfred Adler was the inventor of the term *inferiority complex* to describe the nagging self-doubts that plague some of us. Alfred Adler was originally a follower of the famous Sigmund Freud. The two men were both Austrian and Jewish but there the similarities ended.

Alfred Adler's story

It is unsurprising that Alfred Adler invented the term inferiority complex. Sigmund Freud was the adored firstborn son of a beautiful young mother who doted on him. Alfred Adler was a sickly second child, who had neither the vigor of his older brother or the pampered position of his younger brother. Adler was always seen as the least innovative of the three great founders of psychoanalysis; the others being Sigmund Freud who was older than him and Carl Jung who was younger. Adler remained forever the 'middle brother', a living embodiment of his own theories. Adler struggled with inferiority feelings and Freud and Jung regarded him with condescension. Freud was particularly unkind. Five inches taller than Adler, Freud exclaimed after Adler broke with him to found his own school of psychoanalysis, 'I have made a pygmy great!'

Later, on learning of Adler's death in the small Scottish city of Aberdeen, which had not then achieved fame as the center of the North Sea oil industry, Freud commented unsympathetically that only Adler could manage to die in such an obscure place. In death, as in life, Adler's inferiority accompanied him. When Sigmund Freud's obituary was published in the *London Times*, Freud was credited with inventing

Adler's term inferiority complex. When Carl Jung died in 1961, his obituary in the *New York Times* credited Jung with Adler's idea. Adler was destined to be overlooked.

Early childhood experiences leave us with unconscious expectations. This would be less problematic if people did not respond to our expectations. If we believe we are inferior, we behave in ways that signal this. Other people react to these expectations and behave accordingly.

If we feel inferior to other people, this paralyzes our ability to deal with life's demands. This process starts early in childhood. Consciously or unconsciously, parents can use their kids as a dumping ground for all their disappointments, frustrations and sense of failure. If this is subtly done, it can be more damaging than if it is blatant. Covert operations undermine our sense of security more than a full frontal attack. Negative insinuations, where nothing is ever said overtly and nothing is spelt out fully, give children nothing concrete to react to. There is just an imperceptible undermining. Nothing is ever quite good enough. Nothing we do is ever quite right. A sense of dismay and futility drowns our confidence, leading to a massive sense of inferiority and low self-esteem.

John's story

For years, John's mother complained about his violin practice (unfortunately, the early stages of violin playing are not much fun for the listener). After three years, he gave up. Every time he picked up the violin case, a pained look crossed his mother's face and she asked him how long he intended practicing. Years later, shortly before she died, John's mother asked him why he had given up playing the violin because, 'You were so good at it.' John was so annoyed at this complete rewriting of history, that he could have hit her – but you don't hit 80-year-old ladies. And it did make him realize something useful. He had spent all his life trying to please people who were impossible to please. It was time to give it up.

Not playing the violin has not radically changed the course of John's life – he is not a frustrated musical genius – but it is part of a pattern whereby he suppressed some of his skills, talents and characteristics to please others, especially his wife and mother. John realized that he needed to take a good hard look at himself and became more assertive about who and what he was and what he wanted from life. When an opportunity came at his work for people to take voluntary redundancy with a generous severance package, he decided to volunteer and left to set up his own business.

SHADOW PARENTING

Neglected and rejected children grow up with feelings of low self-esteem. If our parents, who are supposed to always be there for us and to whom we have the closest genetic link abandon us, why should anyone else care for us? Once the pattern of abandonment is set, this may be our unconscious expectation. If it is, we are likely to behave in ways that fulfill it. One study looked at 714 adults hospitalized for depression. The patients perceived their parents to have been hostile, detached and rejecting. These could have been the faulty perceptions of ill people, but this was not the case. Interviews with their brothers, sisters, other relatives and friends confirmed that this was indeed their childhood environment. Depression can be purely physiological in cause, but much depression is due to feelings of low self-esteem. In another study, parents of eight-year-old children were asked to complete a questionnaire about how they raised their children, and their satisfaction with their children and with being parents. A follow-up study ten years later asked the eighteen-year-old children to complete a personality test. Those whose parents had been indifferent or unloving were more depressed.

≋

CHILDHOOD MEMORIES

Childhood memories hold many clues about the person that we are now. Individuals' early memories differ greatly but psychological research shows that particular themes emerge among certain groups of people. Depressed people have early memories of being abandoned and unloved. Anxious neurotic people have frightening early memories. People who have psychosomatic illnesses have early memories of illness. Alcoholics have early memories of powerlessness and of others' being in control of their lives. Criminals have early memories of aggression and violence. Juvenile offenders have early memories of untrustworthy parents who hurt them; as do violent psychiatric patients. These differences in early memories reflect parental and other childhood influences that have helped to make us the people we are today.

The way in which we are treated from birth through those vitally important first years molds and forms our personality and character. How our parents react to us, how our brothers and sisters respond to us, where we come in the family, whether we were wanted a lot or not, all input into these formative influences. Whether we grow up in a happy, stable environment or a dysfunctional set-up, whether parenting was 'good enough', whether we came from a two- or lone-parent family, whether we were brought up by one father, no father or a succession of 'fathers' are all significant influences on our personalities and the characteristics we feel able to show. We should also remember that we are not just products of our environment. The environment reacts with our genetic make-up to create unique individuals. Children experience similar situations and respond to them completely differently. What one child finds challenging, another might find overwhelming. Where one child reacts with resignation and passivity, another might react with rebellion and delinquency. An environment that one child finds supportive and caring might be suffocating to another. We select from a range of potential responses and they become part of our conscious selves. Other responses are relegated and suppressed into the dark side. As we develop conscious personalities that are individual and different, so too do we develop shadows, our own unique dark side.

≈≈

PARENTS

Within the psyche are certain patterns called *archetypes*. 'Mother' and 'Father' are two of these. We are born with unconscious expectations of how parents should behave. They should care for us; they should like us, love us and teach us what we need to know to survive in the world. If we come from dysfunctional families, early on we may realize consciously or unconsciously that our parents do not have the attitudes towards us that we have been biologically primed to expect. We are unlikely to be able to reason well enough or to have the emotional strength as children to decide that there is something wrong with our parents. We are more likely to believe that there is something wrong with us – something that needs to be hidden.

As we grow up and our relationship with our parents changes, the way we view their role in our childhood will also change. Typically, young children think their parents are perfect, teenagers think their parents got it all wrong, then as we get older we come to accept them as human beings with faults. If we become parents, our expectation of what parents can do and be may change drastically. We may take a much more charitable view of our parents' parenting skills when we are faced with the deficiencies of our own. Conversely, if our childhood has been severely dysfunctional, we may realize with even keener insight just how abusive it was when we start to parent and realize that that was not how it had to be. To change the pattern we have been brought up with, we need insight. Unfortunately, this does not always happen. Patterns of emotional dysfunction or abuse can become the norm for children, so then when they become parents themselves, this is how they expect parents to be.

As children, we need to feel secure and free from fear. Part of our shadow will be repressed fears and anxieties that can distort our personalities in later life. If we are insecure, we may repeat the pattern and undermine the security of our own children. Parents can undermine their children's security in a myriad of ways. They can indicate that they prefer one child in the family to others. The rejected child may be scapegoated and find him- or herself carrying the family's shadow. Everything negative that happens is his or her fault. Parents may be dysfunctional people who are unreliable, erratic, drunk, dangerous, or psychologically unstable. If they do not find parenting fulfilling and are frustrated in the role, they may have aggressive feelings towards their children. They may tell their children directly that, 'I wish you had never been born.' Or this could be the unspoken message behind their constant criticism and emotional distance. An overtly rejecting parent can be easier to handle than one who sends out ambiguous signals. They may not want to admit their ambivalent feelings. They pretend to love their children. They may shower them with presents, while remaining aloof, cruel and overcritical. Whatever the child does, it can never be good enough. They may also encourage their children to be dependent on them. Dependent children cannot dare criticize or reject the parent because then they would be alone and unable to manage.

When parents were emotionally deprived in their own childhood, they may be unable to give love but still demand it from their children. Instead of children being dependent on parents, they find the roles reversed. Their parents are grown-up children who are emotionally dependent on them. The child is trapped in a relationship that she or he knows to be wrong and should escape from, but the guilt feelings about rejecting this person who is abusive but so emotionally needy may be too great to bear. Instead, in adult life the child withdraws emotionally, visiting the parents as little as possible and unable to reveal her or his real feelings towards them. Unspoken, the heavy weight of the past prevents the family from ever having an authentic relationship.

⇚⇚

SHADOWS FROM THE PAST – FAMILY LEGACIES

Many of us grow up overshadowed by family events that took place before we were born. We may not even know about them. Many of our parents, grandparents and great grandparents lived through enormous social and political upheavals. Often for reasons of economic necessity, persecution or war, people had to leave their countries of birth. They became enforced migrants, exiles from their own cultures, in countries whose languages they did not speak. Feelings of loss and separation may have been the hidden background to their children's lives.

Other families may have family skeletons that are never discussed – illegitimate children given away for adoption, family feuds that mean some family members are never spoken of again, feelings of resentment and bitterness over wills and legacies, abortions, miscarriages, a child born with serious disability who was placed in a far-away residential home, madness, alcoholism and prison. When there are secrets in the family, children will sense that something is wrong. If these secrets affect their parents' response to them, children will believe it is their fault, not that of their parents. A rejected child or one who is kept at an emotional distance will believe that there is something wrong with him or her. Shame and self-hatred can easily follow.

Suzie's story

Suzie is the younger of two daughters. Suzie never understood why her mother seemed so emotionally distant from her, but had a strong bond with Suzie's elder sister who is ten years older than Suzie. As a child, Suzie became a compulsive eater as she attempted to fill the emotional void. At the age of 30, Suzie entered therapy. She was concerned that while she had scores of friends, she had never had a satisfactory love relationship. She knew her weight was a barrier, but even when relationships started they quickly fizzled out. Suzie sensed that there were problems other than her weight. She had never known intimacy and as an adult did not know how to create it.

The therapist suggested that Suzie needed to talk to her mother about their relationship. Suzie did and discovered for the first time why there was such a large age gap between herself and her sister. Her mother had had six pregnancies in the interim. Four ended in miscarriages and the two babies born alive both died within a few weeks. After the long years of disappointed hope, Suzie's mother had been afraid to bond with baby Suzie. By the time it became apparent that Suzie would survive infancy, the pattern was set.

Suzie's discovery that the problems of her childhood were not her fault helped her let go of the past. A new energy came into her life. She bought a cycle and became a keen distance cyclist and she started training in massage. The massage students had to practice on one another and all Suzie could think of for the first few sessions was an image of her lying on the massage mat looking like a beached whale. She thought people would laugh at her but she found that they didn't. A certain aloofness that had kept people at a distance was beginning to dissolve. Suzie is still a large lady, but she is also fit, attractive and confident. She has not yet found the man of her dreams but she is optimistic.

⁑ Something to try ⁑
'WHAT MADE ME WHAT I AM?'

This is an exercise to help you recall early memories. You will need some quiet time on your own. If you have photographs of yourself going back at approximately five-year intervals, you may find it helpful to look at these before you begin.

1 Close your eyes and imagine that you are going back in time. Imagine yourself as you were five years ago – what you looked like, where you were living, who you were living with, where you were working.

2 Now go back a further five years, and so on. At each five-year stage, visualize who you were then – hair, clothes, home, whom you shared your home with, your name – you may have changed your name due to marriage, divorce, or acquiring or dropping a nickname. Go back in five-year intervals until you come to yourself as a baby.

3 Now you are back to yourself as a baby, think about your early environment. What did your parents tell you about your conception and birth? Were you a wanted child, or a careless mistake? Were you kept and loved by your family? Or were you given away or adopted? Were you the baby your parents wanted? Were you the sex they wanted? Were you physically perfect? Or was something not quite right? Was the birth difficult and did this impact on how your mother reacted to you? Were you the first child and therefore a new experience for your parents? Or were you born to an experienced parent? How old were your parents when you were born? Were they ready for parenthood, or did they think of you as a burden? Were you the first child in the family – or the first of your sex? Were expectations placed on you that your brothers and sisters did not have to cope with?

4 You may feel that you do not know the answers to some of these questions, and it may be true that you do not consciously know, but do you know deep in your unconscious? What do you feel are the answers to those questions, based on your earliest feelings, sensations and memories?

5 Take a piece of paper and write out these questions and your answers. Was your early life overshadowed? What did you feel was inadequate about yourself?

6 Having made a list of the expectations that surrounded your birth, make a list of those that you would like to discard or change. You may have absorbed these ideas, but they are not yours. Negative ideas that have been imposed on you by others are something that you can discard. Remember that your life belongs to you. You are a unique individual and while you cannot change your past, the future can be changed.

☆

FIVE THINGS TO REMEMBER

1 Many of our ways of behaving are formed in childhood. They create patterns for how we act in the future.

2 The patterns may have been right then. It doesn't mean they are now.

3 If your parents didn't love you, it's not your fault.

4 If your upbringing was not ideal, make sure that your child self is not controlling your adult life.

5 If you did not have ideal parenting, this isn't disastrous. A bad beginning can give us the incentive to prove we can do better. Have fun changing your life patterns. Live a little!

4

Adult
dark side

Some days I wake up on the wrong side of the bed in a foul mood. And it occurred to me, really, that every one of us has this little scale inside, you know. On one side there's the light forces, and the other side there's the dark forces of our psyche and our make up and the way we look at the world. And every day we wake up and the scale is a little bit tilted one way or the other. And life is a big struggle to try and keep things in proper balance. You don't have to have so much light that you're just a fool for whatever comes along. But, if the scales tip dark, even a little bit, things turn badly for people and those whom they come in contact with.

President Bill Clinton in a speech to a Gay Rights group,
The Guardian, Saturday October 23rd 1999

We enter the world as helpless infants. If parenting goes well, we develop into mature self-confident adults. If it goes badly, we may find ourselves developing defense mechanisms that become an integral part of our personalities. They are unconscious patterns that we continue to act out even when they are no longer required. Then behavior patterns may reflect unfulfilled needs. We come to adult life with the shadow firmly in place with all its different voices that whisper away in the unconscious to undermine us. Shadow appears in the guise of the doubter. It's the voice that whispers, 'You're no good. You'll never amount to much. People like us can never make it.' It is all those doubting voices that you have heard around you at one time or another and have unconsciously absorbed. If we think we are inferior, we feel bad about ourselves and become paralyzed by feelings of disempowerment. Inferiority feelings lead to guilt, anxiety and doubt. We come to believe that our wishes and hopes are without value and are inhibited from living at our full capacity and achieving the maximum we can within the range of our abilities.

Adult life thrusts us out into the world to sink or swim. We are constantly faced with new challenges and situations where our skills and abilities will be judged. If we have self-esteem, we will see these occasions as opportunities to show what we can do. We know that we may not succeed but we will do the best we can. We are undaunted by failure because we know deep down we are worthwhile people. Sometimes we have not been brought up in ways that give us self-esteem. We have not been encouraged to compete with others, so we never learn the joys of success, of how to cope with not doing as well as we would like, or with other people being better at something than we are. We opt out instead and maybe sink into a life of fantasy. We will win a lottery, be talent spotted by a Hollywood producer, an unknown rich relative will appear and leave us millions, solving all our problems. We will wait forever.

Fear of failure, of not being able to cope with disappointment and of feeling that we would be so worthless if we fail that we cannot live with ourselves, can mean that we never try to achieve. Another strategy is to try, but to sabotage our efforts. This is called *self-handicapping*. Before an important exam or critical business meeting, we stay up so late that we are tired and forgetful in the morning. We put off revising until it is too late. We carry on doing a weekend job in the run up to exams. We displace our anxiety by filing papers instead of preparing an all-important presentation. Rather than try and not do as well as we would like, we do not try at all – and end up doing very badly indeed. We console ourselves that we are just as good as the workaholics, but we are not sad geeks who want to sit indoors all day studying or working our guts out. We have far better things to do with our time. Another classic self-handicapping strategy is to convince ourselves that we are ill before an exam or other important and testing event. We may even manage to make ourselves ill.

Mario's dark side

Mario became so stressed before his final university examinations that he developed abdominal pain and was admitted to hospital with suspected appendicitis. The pain went away, but only after the examinations had finished. He avoided taking the examinations and was awarded (rewarded with) a good degree classification based on his coursework. The avoidance strategy was successful, but long-term the effect was less desirable. By developing illnesses, Mario found that he could avoid all manner of events that he found stressful. He could not attend funerals, be at work during evaluations, or deal with any kind of conflict or argument because he would develop an illness. The avoidance behavior damaged his relationships with others because they felt that he always let them down at crucial moments. By the shadow's usual self-deception, Mario could not see this. He thought of himself as a kind and loving person, which he is, but also as exceptionally solid and reliable. He just happened to suffer from a lot of illness.

SELF-DELUSION

I'm just a soul whose intentions are good.
Oh Lord, please don't let me be misunderstood.

'Don't Let Me Be Misunderstood', The Animals, 1965

As small children, we are uninhibited and express all our qualities – good and bad – freely. Part of growing up is about image management. We learn to present ourselves in the way that is required for the situation. The problem is that sometimes we cease to be aware of what we are doing. We start to believe our own propaganda.

Many people deny that they have a dark side. Yet people are always quarrelling with them about the same things. They make the same mistakes in relationship after relationship. Everyone who ever has any financial involvement with them insists that they are selfish and that other people always lose out. They insist it is nothing to do with them. It is always the other person's fault. Why do people have these deluded notions? It is as if they see themselves in a distorting mirror.

We fail to recognize aspects of our dark side because we have delusions about ourselves. We mistake our vices for our virtues. We all know people like this. It is when we think we are detached and independent but our friends think we are aloof and painfully shy.

It is when we think we are leaders but our friends think we are dominating bullies. It is when we think we are the life and soul of the party and our friends think we are drunken bores. We think we have financial acumen when other people think we are unscrupulous and out for what we can get.

≷/≷

DELUSIONS OF GRANDEUR

Thinking we are worse than others is wrong and distorts our perception of the world. The opposite can be equally problematic. Alfred Adler used the term superiority complex to describe what can afflict those whose environments teach them that they are too wonderful. A superiority complex is a delusion that can be maintained for a surprisingly long time – providing we insulate ourselves against anything that might challenge it.

Charles's story

I (Chris) interviewed Charles when he decided to look for a new job. Charles had made a successful career in a medium-sized marketing consultancy, when he was offered a vice-presidency of a major corporation – one of his clients. He took the job, only to discover that he could not adjust to a large corporate environment. He was used to working in a small professional team. His new job required him to manage a large marketing department through two tiers of managers and supervisors. The marketing consultancy where Charles had worked recruited upper-middle and upper-class students from the best universities. His new organization prided itself on its diversity policies. Charles' staff did not like his management style, his accent or manner.

Nervous in his new role, he retreated into autocracy. Staff were discontent and deadlines were not being met. As the atmosphere deteriorated, valuable staff began to leave. Major rows developed between the President and Charles. Charles began a rapid search for another job.

Charles was miserable when talking about his job, but glowed with enthusiasm when it came to his family. He was the eldest of seven children. They were 'a wonderfully close and supportive family'. Charles 'loved his family to bits' – especially his mother, who emerged as the family matriarch. Charles was 34 and unmarried. Every weekend was spent back at the family home. Charles' mother had told all her children from the earliest age that theirs was the best family in the world. It wasn't too difficult to convince the children of this. They were wealthy – their family was a long-established upper-class dynasty of successful people. Oil paintings of distinguished forebears – lawyers, judges and politicians – adorned the walls of the family home. They had a swimming pool, tennis courts, and Charles mixed all his life with people from the same social background. Together they formed a walled-in clique of people like themselves, reinforcing one another's convictions that they were a social elite.

Charles had never failed at anything. In his last year at university, his classmates voted him 'man most likely to succeed'. He was a brilliant marketing strategist, he told me, and a natural leader. He knew he was a leader because his friends (who were very similar to himself) had told him so. So on this first occasion in his life when things started to go wrong, it couldn't possibly be his fault. The President was obviously threatened by him, jealous perhaps of his superior education and family background.

After being told all his life that he was wonderful, naturally Charles assumed this was true. If a superiority complex is never challenged, it interferes with our grasp on reality. For Charles, it was not until he was 34 and found himself in a job situation that he couldn't handle that any doubts set in. For mortals who are less cushioned than Charles, doubts set in much earlier. If our parents think we are wonderful, special and better than anyone else, we are going to think that we are great. We get used to being 'special', 'wonderful', and the centre of attention at home. We develop the idea that everyone should defer to us, that we are the most important person wherever we go. Then off we go to kindergarten – and a rude awakening. Other people do not see us in that way at all. We are expected to share exciting toys with other children. If we hurt ourselves or get frustrated and cry, our needs may not be attended to immediately. We may have to wait in line instead of being served first. We may have to sleep when we would rather play and play when we would rather sleep.

If we are used to the world conforming to our expectations, what happens when we discover that the outside world is not like that? An instinctive response is to think that there must be something wrong with us, but if our self-esteem is sufficiently high to protect us from this awful notion then we may find another logical answer to the anomaly. We are special, wonderful and different: it's just other people haven't noticed yet.

Psychologists see low self-esteem as bad – and it is; but having high self-esteem does not necessarily make us nice people. Some severely dysfunctional people think they are great. They suffer from *deluded self.* People who value themselves highly may be deluded people who never look behind them at the long shadow they cast.

If we think we are wonderful and others are so lacking in insight they do not notice, then the solution is to find environments where our 'specialness' can be noticed. We may develop a drive to be best at everything – sports, academic work, art, social charm, dance, whatever – but we will be doing it for the wrong reasons. This won't make us happy. We'll be doing it because we want admiration and not for the joy of the activity itself. We may take things a step further onto a platform that for brief moments gives us the adulation we want – the stage. Some performers are addicted to the roar of the crowd. They can never have enough because whatever they do will never be enough to fill the void of that first discovery that not everyone thinks they are as wonderful as they and their adoring parents do.

Another solution is to create an environment where other people are forced to acknowledge our specialness. We become corporate tyrants, or domestic ones. A small minority take tyranny a step further than most. The world is too stupid to recognize their great merits and genius, so it must be forced to sit up and take notice. We get the pathological serial killer who, inadequate in other ways, finds something he can do – and aims to kill more and get more publicity than any other serial killer. Great political tyrants are born from early childhood inferiority feelings. Adolf Hitler was an indifferent scholar, from a poor family background, with an abusive father, a member of a nation defeated in war, with only mediocre talent in the area he most wanted to shine – art. From his point of view, his solution was sheer genius – he would make himself the unchallengeable leader of a nation that he would make the greatest on earth. From this folly, millions died. He achieved what he wanted – fame, a fame that became infamy.

Deluded self often works through what seems like logic. 'Of course, it's not my fault if other people don't like me. It's just because I'm so brilliant that other people are jealous of me.' 'People find me threatening because I am so successful. They criticize me just to undermine me.' 'People are always accusing me of (*insert any negative adjective that seems applicable*) but they are wrong. People don't understand me.' Of course, deluded self's logic is rationalization. If we find that the same patterns of behavior are coming up in relationship after relationship and situation after situation, there is only one common denominator – us. Maybe the world is being unfair to us. Maybe everyone misreads our signals, but they can only read the signals that we are sending out. If people are getting the wrong message about us, then we need to change the message.

⪥

PERSONA AND IMAGE

In childhood, we learn to create a *persona*, which was the term given originally to a mask worn by actors in the ancient theatre. When someone came on stage wearing a hero's mask, then the audience knew that what they were seeing was the hero character. When the same person reappeared with a different mask, the audience knew this was a new character. It is normal to want to present a good impression and to put our best foot forward in certain situations. In fact, there are situations where we are expected to be on our best behavior and to do exactly this. When we first meet our partner's parents, when we go for a job interview, when we ask the boss for a raise – these are all times when we want to look and sound our best. This is fine, providing we know what we are doing. We can walk off stage, take off the mask, and in the privacy of our own homes, with friends, partners and children, we can be our true selves. If we are not aware of the 'real me', we are in danger of thinking that we are the persona. We fall victim to the deluded self.

This does not mean that the persona is not useful. We visit the doctor and enact the role of helpful informed patient. Even if we can see that our doctor is stressed and struggling with the day's work, we can help things along by pretending not to notice and signaling back that the doctor–patient interaction is going well. A lot of this is unconscious. We mutually reinforce each other's personas because it helps social interaction. If we attend a parents' evening to find out why our son is getting poor marks at school, we want to interact with a teacher – Mrs Jones the professional – and not Mrs Jones whose love life is a disaster and would like to talk through her problems with someone. Adopting a persona in work situations is fine. What is not so good is if we mistake our cleaned-up whitewashed persona for the real thing. Deluded self steps in and thinks, 'This is me.' We fall into the trap of being little Miss (or Master) Perfect who always gets everything right. Of course, if you read school stories as a kid, you will know that everyone hates the goody-goody. Perfect people are perfect bores.

The problem with the ideal image is that it is often completely deluded. It is largely based on the reactions of others who may not understand us at all. Our idealized self-image can subject us to a tyranny of *shoulds*. We should do this, be this, believe this. We should study more, exercise more, work harder, get up earlier in the morning, get an attractive partner, and pass our examinations with honors. If we fail in any of these enterprises, we are devastated. We have to be perfect students, employees, bosses, parents. All this may lead to neurotic competitiveness – the need to compete with others and win at all costs. Low self-esteem in childhood creates teenagers and adults whose self-worth depends on their achievements. All over the Western world and in South-East Asia, suicide rates among teenagers have soared. Teenagers kill themselves because they feel they have done badly in exams, and often they are completely wrong; they have done well. They kill themselves because their boyfriend or girlfriend leaves them and therefore they are worthless. So strong are the social pressures to be successful at everything we do, that people whose self-esteem is fragile will decide that life is not worth living if something quite minor goes wrong.

⋚⋛

IMAGE MANAGEMENT

Sociologist Erving Goffman suggested that we live our lives as though we are actors in a play. We present a face to the world, the persona, that we hope will make people like us, esteem us, find us non-threatening, or whatever it is we think we should present as our face that meets the world. We enact an idealized performance and act as though we support and embody idealized social values. We leave clues for others to pick up that signify this idealized view. We wear the right clothes, we use the right language, and we do the right kind of job. We have the prescribed attitudes to study – which may be to study hard or to pretend that we do not study at all, depending on our particular peer group leanings. We engage in *impression management*. This is normal: we want to 'put our best foot forward.'

Impression management only becomes pathological if we do it all the time. This is when the trickster aspect of the dark side is likely to emerge. The dark side trickster will compel us to do something that 'trips us up.' We get drunk at the office party, trap our boss's boss in a corner and bore him or her rigid for half an hour. We come out with a Freudian slip. We mean to tell an important client that the painting in his office is lovely and say ugly instead. The greater the disparity between image and reality, the greater the tension between the two. The greater the tension, the greater the inevitable collapse. It is like the recoil of a giant steel hawser snapping under an unendurable strain.

⤝⤞

THE BURDEN OF INDIVIDUALITY AND CHOICE

Human beings are faced with a tricky psychological problem. We are no longer animals, but have conscious awareness. We have built wonderful civilizations, but our societies have become highly fragmented. We are surrounded by people, but they do not know us. The downside of our great technological advances is that we often feel separate and isolated from others. We also have considerable individual freedom – and what a terrifying prospect this can be. In a society that permits you to do and be more or less anything you wish, how do you decide what to do with your life?

As adolescents, we often adopt a peer group identity in an effort to separate ourselves from our parents and to find out who we are. This becomes part of our adolescent persona. Adolescence is also a time of confusion. What are we going to become? Who are we going to be? Inwardly, we often feel isolated and confused as we make the transition from child to adult identity. We ease our loneliness and isolation by striving to become exactly like everyone else. We dress like our friends, eat the same foods, go to the same hang-outs, listen to the same music, create a slang that defines our group by being incomprehensible to everyone else. Ironically, the more unconventional our outward appearance, the more likely it is that we are seeking a sense of identity conforming to the norms of a social subgroup. If we are instantly recognizable by our clothes as belonging to a particular street gang or group, we immediately have an identity in the world. The problem is that such outward conformity is a trap. People will treat us as the presentation rather than the person behind this. We may lose our true sense of self, but mature adulthood is about becoming what we are truly meant to be.

SWITCHING OFF THE CRITIC IN YOUR HEAD

In order to be what we are meant to be we have to let go of counter-productive thoughts and behaviors so that we can see and think – truly, realistically and clearly. None of us are perfect; most of us find it a struggle to make our way in the world. One solution is to give up. Passive people expect the world to come to them and whatever they want and need to come from outside themselves rather than from their own efforts and resources. Active people know that they have to go out and meet the world. Life is a series of challenges. Sometimes we win and sometimes we lose, but challenges can be fun.

Do you have an inner voice that gives you a critical running commentary on everything you do? What a stupid thing to do! How could you let yourself be fooled like that? God, you look ugly! You deserve to be punished for that. I hate you. And that's on the good days.

Vivianne's inner critic

I only woke up to the inner voice that spends all its time undermining us when I was in my twenties. My training supervisor asked me whether I had a voice in my head that commented on my life. 'I have,' he said. 'It's like a radio commentary. It never switches off.' At first, I couldn't think what he was talking about and then I realized that it was true. An inner negative voice was always doing me down. Like a cross between a bitching sister, wicked stepmother and grumbling grandma, it undermined me every day of my life. It was the voice of shadow – all the accumulated critical voices of parents, teachers and peers of my childhood. There and then, I decided it had to go. I took up meditation and learned visualization techniques. From meditation I learned to be present and focused in what I was doing so that all my attention was focused on doing whatever it was – from washing the dishes to writing a report. And inside there could be beautiful silence.

When we focus, we become absorbed in whatever it is we are doing. Monks and nuns in all religious traditions learn this process, as do shamans, magicians, sportsmen and women, dancers, archers, and people who do extremely dangerous jobs for a living. When our attention is focused, all of our being is concentrated into one-pointedness. We lose our inner fragmentation and become at one with what we are doing.

If you have an incessant internal commentator that rubbishes everything you do, you can learn to get rid of it. Every now and then, it will pop up screaming, 'You stupid bitch!' or 'You sad bastard!', but once you are more conscious of it you can tell it to get lost. 'I don't need you,' is the message. 'OK, so I'm not perfect – so what!' Try visualizing the voice as a ghetto blaster that talks away to itself whether anyone is listening or not. Then press the off button and pull out the plug.

In the Norse mythology of Germany and Scandinavia, the World-Tree Yggdrasil represents the universe. This contains all the different worlds of the universe in all their beautiful variety. It is a wondrous creation, but it is constantly being undermined. A serpent called Nidhögg, Gnawer-from-Below, gnaws at one of its roots, undermining it. A goat gnaws at the leaves so it cannot grow. The serpent and the goat in our own inner world are the voices of criticism and doubt that stop us daring to dream, daring to achieve, daring to be ourselves. At a shadow workshop, a woman told us that her reason for being there was to 'stop beating herself up mentally.' Everyone in the room knew what she meant. We need to acknowledge when we haven't done things as well as we would like, or when we do something wrong, but getting things wrong doesn't make us useless people. This is so important that we should go over it again. 'I get many things wrong, but I am not a useless person.' Shame is a useless emotion when things go wrong in our lives. That doesn't mean we shouldn't face up to our deficiencies, but facing up to things means moving forward, not wallowing in the past. If something goes wrong, it is a learning opportunity. 'What do I change so this doesn't happen again?' 'If I've done something wrong, what can I do to repair the damage?' These are useful questions to ask because they are focused on positive action. The answers may be, 'There is nothing you could have done differently.' 'This damage can't be undone.' Sometimes we do bad things because we have insufficient self-knowledge to do any better. This doesn't mean we can't do better now. We do not have to punish ourselves for the past. We do owe it to ourselves to do the best we can in the future. Don't limit yourself by listening to the negative voice in the head. Instead, allow yourself to be as good as you are. Move out into the future, rather than bottling yourself up in the past.

Negative thinking is strongly linked to shadow. Somewhere in our upbringing, we developed a negative view of the world and ourselves. Shadow takes over, so we see ourselves as mainly shadow. We forget about the good bits. We absorb negative messages. 'Everything I do goes wrong.' 'I am useless.' 'Everyone is against me.' 'I'm so fat and ugly that no one will ever want me.' Even when reality contradicts these beliefs, they can be so deeply entrenched that we ignore contradictory evidence. Such beliefs can be damaging in one-to-one relationships. We can put pressure on our partners to constantly tell us we are lovable, good, wonderful, and that they must never criticize us. Whenever we focus on negative events in the past, we relive our negative experiences and push ourselves into a downward spiral. Depressive thought patterns also affect how we construe events in the present. Depressive people notice the negative aspects of an event and in particular their own negative contributions. They assume that if things go wrong, it must be their fault.

The shadow feeds on self-absorption. We need to think about ourselves in order to evaluate how we are living our lives and where we are going, but psychological research shows that if we think too much about ourselves, we are likely to evaluate ourselves negatively. We dwell on the less-good factors that make up our personality rather than the good things. In line with this, depressed people have been shown to think about themselves much more than non-depressed people. They also suffer from *negative memory bias* and recall negative things that happen to them while forgetting or downplaying positive things.

Too much thinking about yourself is bad for you. This may seem a paradoxical statement given that the whole purpose of this book is to help you think about yourself, but this is not really the case. The aim of this book is to help you think about yourself in constructive ways and to act upon your insights to make yourself happier and more fulfilled. Negative thinking absorbs our energy without taking us forward. It compares us unfavorably with others, present with past, and dreams with reality. Instead of focusing on what we have, it focuses on what we don't have. The shadow is prone to anxiety and negative thought patterns. Negative thinking becomes a habit. The mind becomes used to running in a particular groove and it takes mental effort to break the boundaries to create new and more positive patterns. What is the way out?

⋙ Something to try ⋘
CHANGING YOUR NEGATIVE THINKING

This is an exercise to see if you can recognize negative thought patterns in yourself.

1 Look at these messages.
   - Anything nice I have will be taken away from me.
   - Everyone is against me.
   - Everything is difficult.
   - Everything is my fault.
   - I am inferior to other people.
   - I am not permitted to enjoy myself.
   - I can never get close to people.
   - I can never have what I want.

- I can never succeed – I am a failure.
- I count for nothing.
- I have to do everything myself.
- I must never be angry.

2 These are programmed messages. I hope that not all are true for you, but some may be and you may have other negative thought patterns of your own. Try now to find out the origin of them.

3 Shut your eyes and imagine saying the statements, or actually say them aloud. You may hear a particular voice saying these messages which is not quite your own. Are these someone else's messages – messages you perhaps learned in childhood from a parent, teacher or other authority figure?

4 Take a sheet of paper and write down the messages that most resonate with you. Then write underneath each message, 'Why?'

5 Now think about the question. Why are you not allowed to enjoy yourself? Why do you have to do everything yourself? What early experiences taught you that these statements were true?

6 Now write down some disconfirming evidence. Think of situations in your life where these statements were shown to be untrue.

7 Now think about the statements again. These are negative messages that we can discard. Write out each message that applies to you on a separate piece of paper and destroy it. Tear it into small pieces and throw it away, or burn it or bury it. Remember you are an adult with the power of choice. These messages need no longer apply to you.

SHADOW-DOMINATED THINKING –
HOW TO MAKE IT POSITIVE

When our thinking is dominated by shadow, we can find ourselves in the position of not only constantly judging everything, but also constantly judging everything negatively. Negative beliefs are hard to dislodge because they are survival strategies designed to help us get through life. At some point in our childhood or early adulthood, we will have found them temporarily useful and they will have stuck. These types of mistaken beliefs distort the way we live and interact with others. This does not mean we have to stick with them. We can change.

One of the difficult arts for human beings is the balance between not thinking and planning, and thinking and planning too much; between being foolishly optimistic and a constant worrier. Some people adopt over-optimism as a strategy because they lack confidence. They find it easier not to think about the difficulties of any enterprise they plan, because the difficulties would seem too daunting and they would lack the courage to attempt the task. The problem is that if we refuse to think about obstacles that might get in our way, then we find ourselves in all sorts of messes that were easily foreseeable and could have been avoided if we had had the courage to stop and think.

In our early adult lives, when we are striving to form relationships and to start careers, not thinking too much about difficulties can be helpful. Partly we do not think about difficulties because we do not have enough experience of life to see where they might lie; partly we choose not to think about the obstacles on our path because they would be too intimidating. Once we are a bit older and have a few successes behind us, we can afford to change strategy. We can sit and plan a bit more before acting. We can check that we are doing things that help us achieve the goals we want. We are likely to have clearer and more realistic ideas of our personal life goals. For each job change, career move, relationship development, we can ask ourselves – is this what I want? What are the difficulties of getting there? What can I do to avoid the difficulties? What is the best strategy I can use to get what I want?'

Finding the balance between optimism and realism is one of the challenges of adult life. Notice that we talk about optimism and realism, not optimism and pessimism. Give up pessimism. It's a complete waste of time.

FIVE THINGS TO REMEMBER:

1 If you have repeating patterns in your life and different people get angry with you about the same thing, you are creating the situation. What are you doing?

2 No one likes a hypocrite.

3 If you don't think you have a shadow, you are wrong.

4 Be clear about your motives for what you do – otherwise your shadow will encourage you to engage in self-deception.

5 Self-esteem, the value we put upon ourselves, depends on how well we know ourselves rather than how good we are at presenting an image.

5)

The dark side
of relationships

Human relationships and making them work can be some of the most difficult things in the world for us. We want to relate to others but are afraid of the responsibility and commitment this involves. We want what relationships can give us, but we do not always want to contribute our fair share towards making them work. Relationships can be immensely rewarding, but they are also littered with ambiguity, betrayal, deception, dilemma, hurt, even violence. We want sex but we are afraid of not getting it right. We want physical connection but are afraid of creating ties that bind. We want ties that bind but are afraid of physical passion. We want friendship but are afraid of intimacy. We transfer to new relationships negative patterns of behavior that are based on relationship problems in the past. When we have had negative relationships with our parent of the opposite sex, we may transfer built-up negative emotions from that relationship to other relationships with members of that sex. We hear ourselves saying things like, 'All men/women are ...' When we hear others or ourselves making sweeping negative statements about whole groups of people, be alert – the dark side is at work.

Kelly's dark side

Kelly was the only child of divorced parents, who adored her. She was their little princess, their beautiful little girl. Kelly is still beautiful. If she had been taller, she could have been a model. As it is, she has a successful career as a television presenter.

Kelly's love life was not a success. Her attractiveness got her many lovers, but none ever lasted more than a few weeks. Sometimes Kelly decided they weren't good enough. Sometimes they made their own swift exit out of Kelly's life, usually by never phoning her again. Kelly wondered for a while if she was lesbian or bisexual and tried relationships with women. These lasted longer and finished in less damaging ways. Many of the women stayed her friends, but the sexual side petered out because Kelly didn't really like sex with women. This wasn't the answer either.

In an effort to find out how she could make better relationships, she started attending a series of our workshops. Kelly believes in telling the truth and is very outspoken. 'All men are bastards,' was one of her first statements at her first workshop. The men in the room flinched visibly.

When Kelly did an exercise to discover unrealized aspects of herself, she drew a bedraggled small girl in a white party dress with a ribbon in her hair. The little girl was alone in a corner weeping while everyone else at the party was enjoying themselves. It emerged that Kelly's beloved father, who she thought had adored her, told Kelly one Saturday morning that he was in love with another woman, and left the house never to return. Kelly had been made by her mother to go a children's party that afternoon and was told that she had to pretend that everything was all right. In fact, Kelly did maintain the pretence, but the little girl crying in the corner was how she felt inside.

Kelly's parents' divorce settlement arranged that Kelly would spend every other weekend with her father, but it never happened. Her father's new partner changed jobs and the couple moved hundreds of miles away. A routine was established whereby Kelly spent two weeks' summer holiday every year with her father and his partner. The two weeks were always a disaster.

Kelly's initial outburst at the workshop was a major clue to what was going on inside. Kelly was furiously angry with her father – and that anger had generalized to all men. She expected men to betray her and let her down and, because of the way she treated the men in her life, inevitably that was exactly what they did. A solution for Kelly was often to let them down before they did it to her. Sometimes the need for vengeance against men went further. She had deliberately sabotaged the career of at least two men in her TV network. This had got her the position she had today and her ratings were high enough to ensure she kept her job, but she was deeply unpopular with most of her colleagues and the research staff always made her work their lowest priority, which created considerable extra stress for Kelly at work.

The first stage for Kelly in getting in touch with her dark side was to acknowledge how angry she felt. The second stage was to tell her father how much his behavior in her childhood had hurt her. Kelly hadn't contacted her father for nearly ten years. She was astonished at how difficult she found it to admit how emotionally vulnerable she was and that she needed something from her father, even now when she was 32 years old. She drafted numerous letters and tore them up, imagined countless telephone conversations but couldn't bring herself to pick up the phone, and eventually found out his work e-mail address and sent him an e-mail. Nothing came back for two days and then she received a lengthy reply. It was two pages of self-justification intermingled with self-pitying comments about what a terrible time he had had in his second marriage and how equally dreadful his third (now defunct) marriage had been as well.

To her surprise, Kelly read the e-mail and laughed, and carried on laughing. The father she had adored all her life, whose rejection had blighted her emotional relationships, sounded like a self-absorbed child. She had spent years of her life being angry with someone who just wasn't worth the effort. She also found herself reading phrases that often went through her own mind and which were now mirrored back at her. 'Women always let him down.' 'All three of his wives had cheated on him' – something that in her mother's case she knew to be untrue. Kelly began to think about the pattern of her behavior in her own relationships and didn't like what she saw. She also saw that she was a long way ahead of her father. She could see what she did. He couldn't. She started to wonder for the first time about his relationship with his parents. They had died when her father was in his early teens. Maybe he couldn't really help the way he was.

Kelly's first impulse was to tear up her father's e-mail and never contact him again, but instead she wrote a long and careful reply challenging his statements and telling him something about her own relationships. A tentative e-mail relationship began to develop. Each would write and the other would take some time to reply, but after a few months, Kelly found she was looking forward to her father's e-mails. He began to talk intimately about a new relationship he was trying to develop and admitted that what Kelly had written had made him stop and think. He told her that he now watched her on television every morning before he went to work. He told her how good she was and made perceptive comments about her dress sense and the image she projected. Kelly realized that she had inherited a strong aesthetic sense from her father, as well as copying his less successful behavioral patterns, and that despite her father's faults, he had given her something of value.

Kelly thought a lot about the pattern of her past relationships and realized that she had to take responsibility for their failure. She also realized that it was possible to change the way she behaved. Her father had begun to do so by taking on board what she had told him. She could do the same herself. Kelly joined a dating agency for single professionals and attended a series of parties and group dinners. She found that, as usual, men flocked around her, but she decided to take things slowly. She discovered that she was attracted initially to men who were quite like her father – carefree, fun, but with problems about commitment. She mentally sifted out all these and instead approached a man she found attractive and mentioned she had two tickets for a concert the following week. Would he like to come? Kelly noticed that she was inwardly shaking when she asked him. It was one of the most terrifying things she had ever done. It was the first time that she had ever taken the risk of being rejected by making the first move in a relationship.

Kelly's first date did not prove to be a long-term relationship but ended much as her relationships with girlfriends had done – they parted friends. By now, Kelly had realized that she did not have to be a relationship victim. She could make choices about what she wanted. Shortly afterwards, Kelly found she was attracted to a neighbor who was new to the city. Again she made the first move, inviting him to a large dinner party with other neighbors she thought he might enjoy meeting, but making sure she had enough time for some one-to-one conversation. The evening was a huge success and over a period of twelve months, the relationship has deepened. Kelly would like their relationship to evolve into marriage but she is taking things slowly. In the meantime, she is planning to take a holiday to meet her father for the first time in nearly twelve years.

⋛⋚

BEING OURSELVES

Kelly's inner journey involved facing certain things about her behavior, acknowledging responsibility for them, and acknowledging that she had the power to change them. It also involved a positive realization – that it wasn't her fault that her father had neglected her. As she came to understand her father better, she realized that her father's immaturity had been the problem, not anything she had done. She also realized that she had absorbed negative ideas from her mother. She had not been allowed to show how much she needed and wanted her father. That was part of her that she had to hide away so as not to hurt her mother. It was only in her thirties that Kelly started being herself.

Do you feel inwardly lonely, that people do not understand you and have mistaken ideas about who and what you are? If so, it means you are not showing yourself as you are. And if you are not showing yourself as you are, why not? What are you afraid of? Is your fear of intimacy bound up with a fear of being 'found out', a fear that you might be found wanting? Are you afraid that if people know what you are really like, they will reject you? The problem is that if we conceal part of ourselves, if we never show what we are really like, people cannot form relationships with us, or at least, not real relationships. This is even more of a problem in modern society when sex is often used as a way of getting to know someone, rather than something you do with someone you know. When we are not being true to ourselves and are pretending to be something that we are not, we feel uneasy. We know we are getting it wrong, but we are not sure how. Everything we do seems somehow to slightly miss the mark – which causes more anxiety. Life becomes a frightening road full of dangerous bends and hidden hazards. When we are not at ease with ourselves, other people will not be at ease with us.

We often begin to hide what we are in childhood. There may not be anything wrong with us. It may simply be that we are different from the rest of our family. We will have absorbed messages that some aspects of our personalities are not acceptable. Maybe you were a boy who would have liked to be a musician – but the family ethos was that men have to be responsible and get 'proper career' jobs that enable them to support a family. Maybe you were a girl who wanted to be a doctor – but your family was convinced that marriage and children were much more important for women than careers. If the aspirations that are part of the real you were suppressed early on, then you will not be the person you were meant to be. Friends and lovers will be relating to half a person and not a whole one. When you are able to let yourself be a whole person, then you will be able to enjoy full and authentic relationships.

≷⁄≶

RELATIONSHIPS

We often imagine that sexual relationships operate by different rules from other relationships, but why should this be? If you are a good housemate, you are likely to be a good partner. If you are good at friendships, you are likely to be a good lover, especially if you practice your technique a bit. A lover is someone you have sex with, but the other aspects of relating – caring, sharing and consideration – are the same for lovers as for friends. This may sound a long way from grand passion. Falling in love is nature's way of bringing us together to breed and/or bond. When we are in love, we are in a state of heightened emotional arousal. Emotional arousal colors our judgment so we do not see the whole person who is on the receiving end of our 'in loveness'. Instead, we see what we want to see. Falling in love may have little to do with loving one another as real people. Falling in love is about sexual attraction and being attracted to someone's persona, which corresponds to the image of our love ideal. Being in love will not of itself make you good partnership material.

⌁

THE BRIGHTER THE LIGHT, THE DARKER THE SHADOW

Within the intimacy of one-to-one relationships, we play out some of our darkest impulses. Tensions can build up as we allow our dark side to damage others. We can also engage in wilful blindness that can be as damaging as deliberate aggression. Of course, we do not intend to do these things. More often than not, we fool ourselves into thinking that what we are doing is ok. Many people go through life ignoring the implications of their behavior. They leave a trail of destruction behind them and refuse to turn and see the shadow.

Daniel's dark side

Daniel, a dentist, came to see me (Chris) after a series of unsatisfactory relationships. We began to talk about the concept of shadow and the negative potential within us all. Daniel became distressed, even angry. There is no way he could possibly do anything cruel. Daniel is a great humanitarian. He considers himself an exceptionally good person. He once spent six months as a voluntary worker in Africa and is constantly using his communication skills to raise money for charities that work in Africa's war zones.

Daniel prides himself on his ability to communicate – but somehow it never works out at home. Daniel has been married twice and has had two long-term live-in relationships. The problem, according to Daniel, was that none of his partners could adjust to the needs of his work. They kept on demanding more time with him. Each of Daniel's wives and girlfriends is a successful, powerful and beautiful woman. In fact, Daniel likes only the best – the most intelligent, best-looking, highest achievers he can find. He also has an uncanny knack for spotting people who are seemingly superlatively confident but who underneath are woefully insecure.

Like many men, he is a serial monogamist. He will never leave one relationship until he has another one lined up. Each new woman is flattered that an intelligent, successful, witty, fun-loving, entertaining, well-off, good-looking, caring man like Daniel is interested in her. Interestingly, no one seems to wonder why such a wonderfully caring man is cheating on his partner. Daniel never tells his current partner that there is anything wrong with their relationship. He just walks out – straight into the apartment of his latest conquest. The problem is that none of these women has ever had a real relationship with Daniel. Caring Daniel is interested only in the conquest and not in the intimacy that follows. In fact, intimacy is rather threatening to Daniel. There are too many things about himself that he would rather not see. He terminated the counselling sessions.

$$\approx$$

RELATIONSHIP SKILLS

We can fail to make satisfactory love relationships because we fail to see ourselves as we are. We can also make ourselves the victims of unsatisfactory relationships by failing to see other people as they are. We wail that once we get to know a lover, the person changes. To a certain extent, this may be true. Most of us are on our best behavior on a first date. Then gradually we loosen up and let it all hang out. We start to reveal our endearing eccentricities – like leaving damp towels on the bathroom floor, storing our spare change in the fruit bowl with the fruit, giving up shaving and deodorant at weekends, sneaking cigarettes outside the back door when we are supposed to be born-again non-smokers, leaving the kitchen looking like a teenage party trashed it whenever we make a meal – all the baggage that comes with the wonderful privilege of being our chosen and preferred. However wonderful our partner is, when the 'in love' bit wears off and our vision clears, we are not going to like everything we see.

People often confuse sexual desire, being in love, and loving. We can desire people we dislike. We can be in love with people we barely know. Loving is different. It is real, wonderful and often hard. It develops from deep intimacy and openness. It comes from accepting someone else warts and all and being accepted by them in return. It's only when we reveal our dark sides to one another that we can tell if it's possible to make a real relationship. Sometimes we decide we can live with our lover's dark side; sometimes we can't. The important thing is to be grown up about this and to accept that we have a negative side and so does our partner. Is it a negative side we can live with or not?

⧓

BEING A LOVER AND A FRIEND

It is easy for us to feel sexual love towards another person and equally easy for us to experience the jealousies and possessiveness that are the negative qualities of that emotion. What is not so easy is the art of being a good lover and friend to our sexual partners. The same opportunities for competition or co-operation, for boosting or undermining one another, occur in sexual partnerships as in friendships.

Heather's story

Heather and Stephen were a glamorous couple. At the age of 28, they had all the trappings of success – the right cars, jobs, apartments, friends, connections and career potential. They met when Stephen, a journalist, came to interview Heather, an investment banker, about careers in finance for women. Heather had just broken up from a long-term relationship. Six weeks later, she was engaged to Stephen. What do you do when one of your best friends thinks she is in love with a man that she doesn't really know at all? Heather's friends tried asking a few gentle questions such as – wasn't it a bit soon to think about getting engaged? Didn't she need a bit more healing time from the previous relationship? Why was she convinced that her fiancé was the 'ideal man for her'? Answer: 'Because he has such beautiful blue eyes.'

Unfortunately, Heather's upper-middle-class parents thought Stephen was just as wonderful as Heather did. They were thrilled that Heather had finally grown up and was getting engaged to someone whose parents came from the same social background as theirs. Heather's friends gave up the struggle and went to the brilliant society wedding with an 'Emperor's New Clothes' mentality. Were they the only people who could see that this really was a bad idea? Two years later, the relationship broke up after endless rows. The problem was not that Heather and Stephen were different – they were too similar. Both were good-looking, highly intelligent and competitive. Heather had been brought up as the third child in a family where her siblings were all brothers. Heather was used to men as rivals for attention, personal space and achievement. As the only girl, she had to prove she was better than they were. Stephen was brought up as the eldest of three boys – but only just. His younger brother was two years' younger than him and talented in one area where Stephen had hoped to shine – rock music. Eventually Stephen had admitted to himself at the age of 22 that his younger brother was going to make it, whereas he was not. Stephen was left with a strong desire to achieve in other fields. He became a successful journalist. Heather was a successful investment banker. For Heather and Stephen, competition was in their life-blood. One had to do better than the other. They began to work longer and longer hours – and hardly saw one another. Instead of enjoying one another's popularity and achievements, they both wanted to be the first, the best. Finally, Heather moved out.

Heather is a typical serial monogamist. After a few weeks she was straight into another live-in relationship, this time with Ian, a geologist she has known for years. Heather's parents could not understand why she gave up the glamorous and successful Stephen for someone who drives a beat-up jeep, has no dress sense whatsoever, is less good-looking and is very demanding. When Heather is late home, Ian lets her know what he thinks about that. Instead of working long hours, he prefers her to come home on time for a candlelit dinner (which he cooks – Stephen had never cooked a meal in his life) and sex. When Heather spends hours in front of the mirror deciding what to wear, Ian tells her she's vain and looks sexier in Levis. Ian makes demands on her time and wants her companionship. Unlike Stephen, Ian is interested in her – and not just in someone to admire him. Rather than spending a fortune on clothes, Heather and Ian go on long trekking holidays and have the ambition to visit every country in the world. Heather has started writing in her spare time. Stephen rubbished her first writing attempts – probably because he felt threatened. Ian encourages her and tells her that they're great. Heather has found someone who loves her for what she is – vanity, competitiveness and all – and what she has the potential to be.

Many of us have a competitive streak. Competitiveness is good in many aspects of life but in relationships we are a unit. We compete against the world. We do not compete with one another. If we have not learned good friendship skills, we will want to be superior to our partners. One way is to try and do everything better than our partners can. Another is to try to put them down so they cannot compete with us.

Jo and Matt's story

Jo and Matt met while she was at university and he was a singer in a rock band. Matt seemed glamorous and Jo was highly flattered when he asked her for a date. The relationship deepened. Jo found she was attracted to Matt's carefree attitude to life, which was such a contrast to her family background. She was the only child of a military officer and her family was very conventional. After a year, Matt asked Jo to marry him. She dropped out of university and took an undemanding office job in a insurance corporation while Matt attempted to establish a music career. Matt was unsuccessful and eventually gave up music to become a sales representative for a pharmaceutical corporation. He earned a good salary but his job was boring and repetitive.

Jo's career began to take off. A female boss noticed her potential and sent her on training courses and provided study leave for her to obtain a professional qualification. Her salary overtook Matt's. As Jo's career blossomed, their sex life deteriorated. Matt seemed less and less interested in her. Jo felt depressed and started to eat more than usual. She began to put on weight. At first Matt didn't seem to mind and just said she was more cuddly. After a few months, he started calling her fattie. At first it was just when they were alone, but then it was anywhere, especially in front of their friends, which hurt Jo a lot. When Jo suggested sex, Matt pushed her away, saying that she was too fat. If she wanted him to want her, she would have to lose some weight. Matt began to have violent temper outbursts if Jo discussed her work. She was boring and obsessed with her job, he told her. What had happened to the person he had married? Jo stopped mentioning work and the temper tantrums stopped, but Matt became increasingly critical of everything she did. Her driving was dangerous. Her cooking was unimaginative. Her clothes were drab. The list of Jo's 'faults' was endless. Jo found her self-esteem disappearing. She began dieting and lost weight, then more weight. At first their sex life improved, but then Matt started calling her 'the stick insect'. She was too thin and no fun to be with any more.

In relationships, sex and the withdrawal of sex are often used as weapons, and criticisms of our partner often disguise what is really the matter – something we do not want to admit. In Matt's case, he could not admit how jealous he was of his wife and that he felt his male role was being undermined. Instead, everything was Jo's fault. Jo did not have the self-confidence to challenge Matt's behavior, even though she sensed what was wrong. Jo and Matt's marriage ended finally in divorce when Jo started a relationship with a work colleague who was not threatened by her success. Matt remarried almost immediately afterwards to a woman who wanted a family and was uninterested in a career.

When we put our partners down in order to enhance our own egos, our dark side is at work. Putting people down is also associated with power and control. We are afraid of their personal empowerment, so we seek to undermine and diminish them. We try to 'cut them down to size', so that we can feel bigger, stronger and more powerful.

⋙⋘

POWER AND CONTROL

Relationships are playing fields for all manner of power games. Often we learn these patterns from our parents and the way in which they manipulate their children or one another. Abusive parenting teaches us distorted messages about love. It also teaches distorted messages about power and control. Ideal parenting creates safe space for children to grow. As children grow, the space needs to become wider, until the whole world is their space and any boundaries they set are their own and not other people's. If we have suffered from abusive control in our childhoods, we can go in one of three directions. We can make sure no one is ever in control of us again by avoiding situations where we are under other people's control. In relationships, we may find it difficult to commit. Alternatively, we can make sure that no one is ever in control of us again, by making sure that this time we are the ones in control – we seek to have power over others, or we can replicate the childhood situation and look for someone to control our lives for us because we have never learned to control them ourselves. In other words, we can seek avoidance, dominance or submission.

Avoidance may be a less damaging reaction to issues of power and control than some, but it can limit our life chances. Are you someone who drops out of relationships as soon as the other person gets serious? Withdrawal is a way of protecting ourselves. If we do not need other people then they cannot touch us. We do not seek satisfaction of emotional needs and therefore we cannot be hurt or rejected. This path has a high price. We castrate our emotions and so lose part of ourselves. Detached personalities need to maintain emotional distance from others. They strive to become self-sufficient and to experience no extreme feelings towards others at all. They will maintain their privacy at all costs and if they enter a relationship are unlikely to make it succeed because they will never allow their partner to know them sufficiently well. The question, 'What are you thinking?', seems a huge invasion of privacy.

We all have power – power to make choices, energies that we can harness, the will to do things that we want to do. Being powerful means being responsible for the choices that we make and that can be scary. In Western society, we have enormous freedom to decide how we want to live our lives. This means that we can make decisions.

It also means we can make mistakes and get things wrong. Power is a problem and one solution is to give our power to someone else. We can hand over our choices to a person or organization that will tell us what to do. Authoritarian organizations such as the army and some religious groups can do this for us. So too, can a dominant marriage partner.

We can try to find someone else to take over the tricky problem of running our lives for us, or we may go in the opposite direction and find someone else's life to control. We need to be in control of other people's lives when we are not confident of being in control of our own. Most of us are sometimes distant and detached, sometimes controlling, and sometimes willing to be directed by others. In other words, we are flexible and can adapt ourselves to different situations to meet their demands. Flexibility requires openness. When the shadow is in control, we are closed and 'uptight'. One mode of being – detachment, compliance or aggression – takes over and we are unable to let go even when it destroys our relationships. We are compelled towards the overriding tendency and sacrifice everything else to it.

Frances' dark side

Frances is a Catholic but her husband left her and she was forced to divorce. Although she had never had children, her model was the Madonna, the archetypal mother – all-suffering, ever-loving, and absolutely perfect. You needed help with your wedding arrangements – in stepped Frances. You were ill and needed some shopping done – Frances was there like a shot. A broken love affair? Frances was the expert. If you had a problem, Frances was there rooting for you. She hugged you, loved you and plied you with cake. And she prayed for you. Frances belonged to a healing circle, a prayer circle, and three befriending schemes – one for the bereaved, one for seniors, and one for the mentally ill. The whole of Frances' life was about helping others. Why?

Frances fed like a vampire on other people's misfortunes. Her face would light up when someone told her that he or she had a problem. The more problems people had, the more needed Frances felt. Frances' life changed when she decided to take a logical step for someone who wanted to help others – she decided to train as a therapist. This involved three years in therapy, during which she worked through her anger with the husband who had abandoned her and her own lack of self-esteem. She admitted to herself that she was at least partly responsible for what had gone wrong with her marriage. Her husband could not cope with the amount of control Frances exerted over his life. It was like being married to a domineering mother.

Therapy also helped her see that she needed to achieve more. She had married early and had no educational qualifications. To realize her ambition to become a therapist, she took a degree through a distance-learning institution. She was bitten by the learning bug, ending up with a Masters degree. Her ideas about helping also changed. She realized that an important aspect of helping was about showing people that they had the strength to help themselves. Frances' previous helping was to make people dependent on her so that she would feel strong and needed. Frances became a successful therapist and workshop leader. Having explored and worked through the reasons for her own damaged life, which originated in a violent and abused childhood, Frances is a classic wounded healer. She has been there and back again, and can help others make the inner journey too. Frances has ceased being everyone's mother. She is now a wise friend.

✧ Something to try ✧
LOVER AND FRIEND

This is an exercise to help you explore how you relate to others as lover and friend.

1 Take some paper and a pen. Think for a while about the history of your sexual relationships. Who were the three most significant lovers in your life? 'Significant' can include significantly good lovers and significantly bad ones.

2 Write the names of your three most significant lovers on three separate pieces of paper.

3 Now answer:
   - What were the good things about your partner and about the relationship?
   - How did you behave in the relationship – what did you give, what did you take, what did you like about the way you behaved, what did you dislike?
   - What were the bad things about your partner and about the relationship?
   - Once you have covered all three relationships, consider the three together:
   - What did you learn from these relationships – about yourself, about others, and about relationships in general?

4 Take a fourth piece of paper and write down the name or names of up to three people whom you might have liked to have a relationship with but did not. For each one, write down why you did not pursue the relationship. Was it because it was

impractical – circumstances kept you apart, or perhaps they were already committed to someone else? Was it because you did not show them you were interested? If not, why not? Did you rate yourself as likely to fail, or unable to meet their standards?

5 Now think about your current or most recent relationship. What is the negative side of this relationship? Are there patterns emerging that have happened in earlier relationships? Are there any negative feelings that hold you back from having the type of relationships you would like? Can you recognize these feelings in the relationships that you have had before or would have liked to have had, but did not?

6 Write down all the positive qualities that you have to offer to someone as a friend and lover, and what you can bring to a relationship. Also, write down things that you might like to change about yourself to be a better friend and lover.

Friendship skills are learned in our earliest years from our relationships with other children – friends and siblings. Our early experiences of interactions with our brothers and sisters will affect how we interact with peers and colleagues in adult life. A friend should be an ally – someone to share our hopes and fears, joys and sorrows, without fear that he or she is secretly undermining us, competing with us, or enjoying our discomfort or misfortune. Friends are people we trust and who trust us. We may not always see eye to eye, but we feel confident that when we need them they will be there for us.

If we really care about people then we want good things to happen for them and we do not feel diminished by their gains. Their gains are our gains too: it is a win–win situation. Unfortunately, it's not always like that. Dark side jealousy can leak out that takes secret pleasure in others' misfortunes. People enjoy reading gossip magazines not only because they allow us to vicariously experience lifestyles beyond our reach, but because they tell us about the misfortunes of our sporting heroes, glamorous film stars and political leaders. *Hello!* is a UK gossip magazine with the uncanny knack of publishing leading articles about famous couples who break up shortly after the *Hello!* photo shoot. The 'curse of *Hello!*' is a major part of the magazine's attraction.

Tensions and rivalries with friends are reflections of early tensions and rivalries with siblings and childhood friends. Here are some strategies to think about. Do you recognize yourself in any of these?

	Friend wins	Friend loses
Self wins	Your friend succeeds at something, so it inspires you to try harder to succeed = *positive competition enabling self and other*	You don't want your friend to be better than you, so you discourage his/her aspirations = *negative competition limiting others*
Self loses	You don't try to succeed because you will lose the friendship if you become better than your friend (this makes it hard to get out of the ghetto). You play down your abilities through false modesty = *empathic underachievement*	You collude with your friend in underachievement and drag one another down = *shan't play, won't play, refusing to compete and opting out of the game*

Our shadows can seduce us into undermining our friends in all sorts of ways, some of which seem deceptively positive. We fear that if our friend goes to university and we get a job, then she or he will no longer be interested in us. We say university is difficult, elitist – she or he will feel uncomfortable and it will be difficult to make friends. University is expensive, it will mean borrowing money and getting into debt – and many graduates have difficulty in getting jobs. In others words, we think of all sorts of excuses and barriers other than the true one – that we are jealous and afraid of losing a relationship that is important to us.

The shadow can make us undermine our friends in all sorts of ways, but measuring ourselves against others is not negative in itself. It depends on what we do next. Competitiveness can be positive – if it inspires us to do something that we can achieve. Our friends' successes do not mean that we have to emulate their achievements in exactly the same field. If competition makes us aim for goals that are not our own, then we will waste time expending energy on things that are not important to us, simply because we want to keep up with someone else. This is a lose–win situation. Our friends are winning because they are achieving what they want to achieve. We are losing because we have been diverted off our course. However, competitiveness can be win–win if it inspires us to do what shadow's self-doubt has never allowed us to do.

Vivianne's story

As a 'head in the clouds' person who is not always aware of the physical world, brought up in a home where my mother did not drive and believed that women drivers were bad drivers, it was not easy to convince myself that I could pass the difficult British driving test. Two things propelled me to try. Chris acquired a company car that he did not need to go to work and this beautiful, elegant, shiny vehicle was sitting in the drive tantalizing me as I walked to the shops every day. Then a particularly daffy dancer friend took ten driving lessons and passed first time. On the principle that if she could do it, I must be able to do it, I got myself a woman instructor – an important point as I needed a role model, and if Chris had taught me it would have brought out all the worst in his dark side – and passed. The instructor was good but not entirely helpful. I made the mistake of telling her I was a psychologist and spent ten lessons advising her about her complicated love triangle while driving through London traffic. Still, it improved my concentration no end. My friend's success inspired me. This was win–win because I wanted to pass my driving test.

When some of our friends bought houses abroad – one of my favorite fantasies since I was very young – it made me realize that this dream could be turned into reality. As I sit in my house in France writing this, I know I might never have had the courage to live out the dream if someone else had not been a pioneer.

❖

THINKING ABOUT RELATIONSHIPS

You have now thought about relationships and about how you behave within relationships. You may have seen patterns that you tend to repeat. Some of these patterns may be positive, but some of them may be negative patterns that you would like to change. Remember that loving is an art and skill. Our dark sides are not only about negative aspects of ourselves that we want to hide. They are also about positive aspects of ourselves that somehow do not match our self-image. People are often reluctant to allow their self-image to grow and evolve. Ruts are safe places to be. They are also shaded places. Real adult relationships, however, require openness.

Russ's story

Russ came to see me (Chris) because his wife told him he was uncaring and cold. He was mystified. He loved his wife intensely, they had a good sex life, he spent all his leisure time with her and their children, rarely spent money on himself, and was constantly improving their home. 'How often do you tell her you love her?' I asked. Russ looked extremely uncomfortable. No, he didn't go in for that sloppy stuff. His wife knew he loved her – look how much he did for her! He wouldn't do it if he didn't care. Russ came from a family of five brothers with a father who they knew cared about them, but never said so. Learning to tell people what he felt was a completely new experience. And he had to learn that expressing his feelings did not undermine his masculinity.

Russ agreed to an action plan. (Russ was essentially an action-oriented person, so he liked the term. It made what he was doing seem practical and real.) In future, Russ would have the store wrap his wife's birthday present in nice paper rather than giving it to her in a plastic bag with the receipt in case she didn't like it. He would tell her when she looked nice, and he would get a babysitter once a month and would go out to dinner with her, without the children. Getting him to tell her often that he loved her was slightly more difficult than extracting teeth – but we got there in the end. Russ was astonished at how much their marriage improved – and their already satisfactory sex life got even better.

Men can find it especially difficult to articulate their feelings and some appear to think that having said 'I love you' once when they proposed, or when they started a serious relationship, or even the first time they had a shared orgasm, then that will do. 'She knows that now, so I won't have to say that again' seems to be the attitude, but this obviously is not enough. Some men look mystified when urged to articulate their feelings more. 'But she knows I love her. I wash her car every Saturday – and I do the shopping!.' If this is as far as your romanticism gets take a deep breath and say what you feel – the more you do it, the easier it gets – and demonstrate your love by doing things – but make sure they are the right things. Do not, whatever you do, buy her a set of matching saucepans to show her how much you love her. Buy her luxuries, things you know she likes rather than those you like – and write 'I love you' on the gift tag. What you give conveys how you see the person to whom you give. For a gift to say 'I love you', it is best if it does not remind your partner of the least romantic aspects of her life. The words, 'I love you' are a miracle when they are spoken in sincerity from one human being to another. Gestures in the form of the daily acts that surround a loving relationship, such as the unexpected cup of coffee or tea brought when we obviously need it but have not asked, the bath run when we return exhausted from a long working day, a spontaneous gift – these come from a movement of giving. When we love, we give. Try it.

FIVE THINGS TO REMEMBER:

1 To love someone and care for them, first you have to love and care for yourself.

2 Communicate about problems that are troubling you even if they are unrelated to the relationship, because they will affect your relationship. Shadow is afraid to admit problems such as debts, poor work performance, a difficult boss, because we feel we should be able to cope on our own. The old saying of our grandmas, that a problem shared is a problem halved, is usually true. Friends and lovers are an information resource of experiences and ideas. Learn to ask others for advice. If your friends or lovers aren't interested in your problems, it may be time to change friends or lovers.

3 Long-term loving partnerships are built on true friendship, but remember also to take time to be sensual with each other, enjoy the physical.

4 Don't sulk when offended – discuss what's upsetting you. Sulking is passive aggressive shadow. The message is, 'You made me unhappy, so I'm going to make you miserable until you plead with me to stop.' This is lose–lose behavior. We're losing out because we're not tackling the real issue. We're losing out because of the way our partner is likely to respond. If he or she gives in and panders to our childishness, we are establishing a negative pattern for the future. If our partner doesn't give in, we're both in for a miserable time.

5 Don't demean your partner in private or public. This is shadow one-upmanship where we need to feel superior to our partners, so we demonstrate our superiority by telling amusing anecdotes about his or her failings or through a straightforward aggressive putdown. Ask yourself why you have to put your partner down. What's really going on here?

6)

Body and
your dark side

We have to relate to others. We have to relate to the material world. We also have to relate to our own personal material vehicle – our body. Unlike animals, we do not feel wholly integrated. We have mind and body, thinking and feeling. We have many opposites that we are constantly seeking to reconcile. Factors such as parental upbringing, social conditioning and religious traditions may teach us that one pair of these opposites is the right one and the other is wrong. One polarity is to be fostered and developed and the other should be suppressed and ignored.

Many people go through life oblivious to their bodies – until something goes wrong. It's a bit like driving a car. Unless you are a maintenance enthusiast, you probably think about your car only when you need more oil or gas, the car needs a wash, it's time for an annual service, or it breaks down. Your car probably does get a regular service, but do you? Do you notice much about your body? What kind of fuel are you expecting your bodily engine to run on?

Are you helping your body or hindering it in efforts to provide a housing for your spirit? Do you like it? People often make more fuss of their pets' bodies than their own. Neglected bodies become unhappy and sick bodies – it's partly their way of drawing attention to themselves.

Surprisingly, something as nebulous sounding as the unconscious mind has strong links to the body that bypass the conscious mind entirely. Sometimes body and unconscious mind are in a happy alliance of which we are completely unaware. Unconsciously we are afraid of doing something and body helpfully manufactures an illness that stops us doing it. An important starting point in accessing shadow is to start taking notice of our bodies. Many of our moods relate to things to do with the body. Our eating and drinking patterns, as well as any prescription or other drugs we take, will all affect our moods.

⩘ Something to try ⩘
SHADOW MOODS

Here is an exercise to help to become aware of your moods.

1 Keep a mood diary for a month to get in touch with your bodily moods. Divide the day into four – morning, afternoon, evening and night. Note down everything you eat, drink, and any drugs you take. Note whether you walk anywhere and whether you take any exercise. Note how many hours of the day you are indoors or out, and how much natural daylight you are exposed to. Note your sleep pattern and how long you sleep and whether you dream. Also record in your mood diary your emotional state during each part of the day and anything that triggers a change.

2　At the end of the month, look back and see if you can distinguish any patterns. Are there phases in your hormonal cycle when you feel more vulnerable, less robust, more likely to lose your temper, or are irritable for no reason? Do you feel better if at lunchtime you go outside for a walk? Do you become depressed if you are not exposed to sufficient daylight?

3　Once we have noted these patterns and become aware of when they are likely to occur we cannot cease to experience the hormonal fluctuations, but we can change how we react to them. We can learn to detach ourselves and become independent of them. We can say, 'I am not my moods. I have moods and am aware of them. Sometimes I give in to them; sometimes I do not. I don't always have a choice, but often I do.'

4　We can also learn to manage our moods. If you find that coffee makes you irritable but you enjoy it, only drink it for a certain period each day. If you find you are more relaxed if you go for a walk at lunchtime, start making this part of your daily routine. Show your body that you respect it and are interested in it. Your body needs what a pet dog needs – good food, attention, grooming, health checks and regular walks. In starting to acknowledge the body rather than ignoring it, we are starting to make a stronger conscious link with part of ourselves. As we recognize one part of ourselves, it becomes easier to access others.

ANOREXIA – DENYING OUR EXISTENCE

Many people feel alienated from their bodies. They may want to escape from them. This problem has grown more acute in our media-dominated age when we are constantly confronted with images of unattainably perfect bodies. Our clothing means that we have to expose much more of our bodies than previous generations and at the same time our unhealthy lifestyles may mean that even when we are young we feel ashamed or embarrassed about what we have to expose. Shadow can make us hate our bodies and try to deny their existence altogether. One way of denying the body is through anorexia.

Alfred Adler believed that we all suffer from inferiority feelings to some extent. We constantly compare ourselves with ideals – whether of appearance, personality, material wealth, career success, the type of children we have. Inevitably, reality suffers by comparison. This is why debate rages about the depiction of women in women's magazines and of the images created by supermodels. 'One can never be too thin or too rich,' said Wallis Simpson, whose relationship with King Edward VIII of Britain forced his abdication in the 1930s. Today, with the assistance of make-up, smoking, clothes, personal trainers, plastic surgery and retouched photography, media stars and models create impossibly slender images of perfection; impossible, that is, for any normal woman. The pressure to achieve an impossible ideal causes increasing numbers of young women to suffer from eating disorders such as anorexia and bulimia. Once young women were the main victims of this disease, but it is now increasingly common among young men too. No wonder that this pressure results in feelings of inferiority which can lead to guilt; 'I am not how I should be, I am to blame.' The slippery slide into anorexia begins. In the fantasy world, things can be whatever we want them to be. In reality, we have to come to terms with the fact that perfection belongs to the gods – and we are not gods. Nor are we demons, we are simply human – faults, cellulite, flabby bits, and all. The idea that we are not good enough can lead us to punish ourselves endlessly. It can lead to paroxysms of guilt every time we make a mistake. We have fantasies about being beaten – maybe we even go down the dangerous path of finding someone whose own inner darkness makes them want to dominate and hurt people to collude in a sado-masochistic relationship.

CONTROLLING THE BODY

Anorexia is not only about hatred of the body. By becoming as thin as possible, we reduce the size of our bodies and the amount of space we occupy in the world. In environments that are abusive, this can be a strategy of escape. The less there is of us, the less there is to punish and abuse. We make ourselves as small, insignificant and non-threatening as possible so any danger will pass over us and go away.

Anorexia can also seem a positive strategy in other ways. In situations where we are dominated by others, or we feel our lives are not in our control – a common situation in adolescence – our eating patterns are something we can control. Anorexia can be a way of rejecting over-intrusive parents – we will not accept their food. In situations that are abusive or where our relationship with parents just isn't working, our body image is the one thing we can control and they can't. It may be the only thing that we feel is truly ours – so we make it look the way we want. Unfortunately, if we are suffering from anorexia and we look in a mirror, we don't see what we really look like. We see ourselves as fat when in reality we are skeletal, but we don't care. Our ability to control what we eat gives us power, but it is a dark side power, a power that can destroy us.

⌇⌇

OBESITY – FILLING THE VOID

When we are 'overshadowed' we are unlikely to feel loved and lovable, but one of the basic human needs is for love and acceptance. Inside us is an inner void that needs to be filled. In Tibetan Buddhism, one of the 'worlds' or states of being on the wheel of life shows beings that are known as 'hungry ghosts'. They are distorted creatures with huge stomachs and tiny mouths. To fill their huge stomachs they must constantly eat. This is our pattern when we are trying to fill an inner void. It becomes impossible to get enough love, reassurance, or applause. A way out is to numb the pain. Food, drink, drugs or sex can be frantic attempts to fill a gap that can only be filled by something completely different – our own self-esteem.

Understanding the concept of the shadow can help to restore self-esteem that may have been damaged by perceiving our body image to be negative. It can also help us understand why we over-eat. Eating can be a substitute for both sex and love. If we feel unloved, we may try to nurture ourselves in counter-productive ways. We are biologically programmed to look to our parents to nurture and care for us. Human babies and most other baby mammals such as kittens and puppies have large eyes and pupils that make us respond unconsciously to them with feelings of love and protection. We are drawn to them and feel that we have to do things for them. As babies, we are programmed to elicit these responses from those around us. If parenting goes wrong and we do not get the right response, we may try to provide it for ourselves. We may try and nurture ourselves by feeding ourselves, especially with sweet things that both give a quick physiological high through a sugar rush in the bloodstream and also pamper – but don't satisfy – the deprived child within us.

Not all obesity is due to deep psychological causes. Obesity can be genetic. It can also start from faulty eating habits as parents feed their children poor quality nutrition and the child eats more and more to counteract deprivation of essential nutrients. Once the pattern is set, it can be difficult to eradicate. The body thinks it is starving because it is missing certain essentials and is constantly signalling us to eat in order to try to get them; but since we keep eating non-nutritious food, we do not give our bodies what they need and the starvation signal remains jammed in the 'on' position. The body is signalling SOS but it is as though we do not know Morse code and cannot read the signal.

If you have been emotionally damaged as a child, then you may have a damaged body image. If you want to change the way your body looks, you will need to work from both outside and inside. Changing body images requires us to accept ourselves, to love ourselves, to respect ourselves. If you start by befriending your shadow, you will have a good place from which to begin.

WHAT ABOUT BODY FLUIDS?

Many people have difficulty in accepting their sexual selves. For women the shadow self is often bound up with shame about the body. Whole generations of women have been taught that their sexuality, bodily secretions and sexual smells are shameful rather than erotic, are a threat to cleanliness and purity rather than a part of healthy biological functioning. Menstruation has for many women been associated with negative images. These types of taboos and folklore teach women to be ashamed what should be joyous. Major problems in couple relationships centre around remarkably few things and communication, or lack of it, is at the root of most. Even though we live in a society that can seem emotionally open and sexually uninhibited, the reality of many people's lives is very different. If you have no experience of positive relationships in your life and have not observed other members of your family in positive relationships, then you may need to learn how to make successful interactions with others, and even if your own parents' relationship works well for them, copying it may not work for you.

Axel and Tanya's story

Axel's German mother was a fanatical housekeeper. She did not have a paid job and every part of the house was cleaned every day. Axel's father had joined the military straight from school and loved everything to look clean and orderly. Both parents belonged to a strict Protestant denomination and had originally met at a Christian event put on by the local German community where Axel's father was stationed.

Axel was twenty and had had few girlfriends before he met Tanya – his life was dominated by study. When he met her, he was still a virgin. Tanya was a 22-year-old Australian who was spending two years traveling around the world after university. She was more sexually experienced than Axel, but not much. Visa problems meant that while Axel and Tanya's romance was blossoming, time was running out. She could not get a visa extension and Axel was in the middle of medical school and could not relocate to Australia. Eight months after they met, they got married and Tanya got residency status. Tanya got herself an office job and with Axel's part-time job and assistance from his parents, they could manage financially. They rented a one-bedroom apartment and settled down to married life. Axel spent long hours studying and working. Tanya's job was relatively undemanding so they fell into a routine whereby Tanya did the shopping, cooking and day-to-day cleaning.

Axel's father frequently praised his wife's cooking and housekeeping abilities, but Axel had never observed any other displays of affection between them. Nevertheless, he knew that they had a very happy relationship. His parents always bought one another gifts for birthdays, anniversaries and Christmas, but they were always practical. His father liked DIY and garden tools or clothes and his mother liked useful items for the home.

On Tanya's first birthday before they were married, Axel bought her a leather handbag. On her second birthday, he bought her a steam iron. He appreciated the trouble she took in ironing his shirts every morning and thought the steam iron would make the job easier. To his astonishment, she burst into tears. He asked her what was the matter and she burst out with, 'Everything!' He was uncaring. He never noticed her appearance. He never asked her how she felt. He never said that he loved her. All he cared about was his medical studies and he was barely interested in her sexually. Before they were married they had sex every night – and sometimes in the morning as well. Now they had sex once a week at the most. Wasn't this abnormal when they were a newly-married couple? Although she liked his parents, she hated having to see them every Sunday. It was their only free time and she wanted them to spend time alone.

Axel was bewildered. He was happy with his new married life and assumed that Tanya was too. He worked hard because he was doing it for them, he shouted, for their future. Did she want to go on working in that dead-end job for the rest of her life? He wanted to get a good job on graduation so they could start a family and she could give up work. But I don't want to give up work, was her reply. How about me – my career? Career? It had never occurred to Axel that Tanya wanted a career. She had said nothing to him about wanting a career. Tanya's birthday ended with Axel sleeping on the sofa in the lounge.

The next morning Axel went to university in a state of shock. He wondered whether to skip classes that day and go to see his mother to ask her advice, but he realized that this was the wrong thing to do. His loyalties were to Tanya now and he had the uncomfortable feeling that his mother might be secretly pleased he was having problems. This thought made him feeling horribly guilty. Axel was taking my (Vivianne's) course as part of his studies. At the end of the class, he plucked up courage to ask if he could talk to me about his marriage. From even the briefest conversation, it was obvious that Axel loved Tanya very much. Axel was very cautious and for him, marrying Tanya was taking an enormous risk. He knew they would have difficult years financially until he finished his studies and that getting married at the age of 21 was a gamble anyway. His parents had been against it and tried to dissuade him, but for the first time in his life he wanted something different from their aspirations for him. He had stuck to his guns, but unconsciously he was afraid that they might be proved right. Maybe it was a big mistake after all.

I asked Axel to list of all the things that Tanya was concerned about regarding their relationship and we talked some of them through. 'How often do you have sex?' I asked. Axel blushed and admitted that it was down to less than once a week. Axel gave all sorts of reasons why this was, including the obvious one that he was often tired, but it didn't quite make sense. Eventually he admitted that the most important reason was that he was terrified of Tanya becoming pregnant. This seemed an odd fear. Surely a 21st-century medical student must know about contraception? However, it seemed that Axel couldn't manage to get condoms on without losing his erection, that knowing all the risks of the pill, he didn't want Tanya to take it, she had difficulties inserting a cap and that they were using the withdrawal method – which explained Axel's worries about pregnancy. Further discussion about Axel's home life made it sound odd too, odder than Axel realized. In the lack of discussion or display of emotions, the sexually stereotyped roles of his parents, and a puritanical attitude to sex, it seemed like something from 50 years ago.

Axel's problems were way beyond anything that could be handled in a post-class discussion so I referred him to the university counseling service. Towards the end of the academic year, he came to see me to say that his marriage was now blossoming. Tanya was studying for a part-time MA in evening classes and Axel now visited his parents on Wednesday evenings while Tanya was at her classes, which cut their joint Sunday visits down to once a fortnight. This was good but it didn't explain fully why Axel looked so happy. 'And is everything else all right?' 'Oh, yes,' blushed Axel. 'The counselor suggested I told

Tanya at least three times a week that I loved her and she suggested a book, you know a sex book. I hadn't realized that women liked, well, some of the things in the book. Yes, er, I just wanted to say thanks.'

Men from a traditional religious background may find it difficult to accept women's sexuality. On the one hand, they want a partner who is an attractive, sensual woman who wants them sexually. On the other hand, their religious teachings will have programmed them to believe that women with active sexual appetites are whores. When it comes to marriage, men from traditional backgrounds whose own mothers do not seem sexual will find it difficult to accept a wife's sexuality. They will be drawn to women who do not express their sexuality overtly and thus are 'good' women. At the same time, they will want the sexy siren of male fantasy. There are a few possible solutions open to this type of man. The easiest ways out are to use pornography or to have affairs. Many men of older generations saw affairs and prostitutes as sexual outlets that saved their wives from being troubled by their unwanted desires. Instead of men and women making whole relationships, they created relationships whereby wives acted as housekeepers and child raisers in exchange for social benefits such as the status of marriage, children and a home, and other women serviced their men's sexual needs. Fortunately, our societies are moving away from this pattern as we realize that the needs of men and women are not so different. All human beings, regardless of gender, have needs for companionship, acceptance by another for the whole of their being, sexuality, and intimacy.

There is a wonderful scene in the gangster soap *The Sopranos* when the hero Tony talks about his enjoyment of oral sex. And could his wife give him oral sex? Tony screws up his face in disgust.

That is the mouth that kisses his children! Killing people is ok, is the message, that is part of his job, but oral sex with one's wife is not. When we divorce body and soul, sexuality and love, respect and intimacy, then we compartmentalize ourselves. Unintegrated, we cannot grow to be whole people. Shadow is separated from ego and we become less than we are. For Tony Soprano, his wife is also the mother of his children. As a mother, and he is a Catholic, she is also Madonna, and the Madonna is ever-virgin. The Catholic Church's archetype imagery of woman creates a difficult and complex scenario for the Catholic-culture man to negotiate. Sex for procreation is good; it belongs in the light. Sex for fun is bad and is pushed firmly into the dark side. Suppressed in the dark side, sexual desires grow in twisted and perverted forms. Seeking expression, they manifest in deception and hypocrisy or worse, into abuse, perversion and violence.

Many religious teachings have encouraged us to be ashamed of our sexual needs. In the days before contraception, societies sought to protect themselves against social instability caused by unwanted children. The easiest way to do this was to make sure that people married as early as possible so their adolescent hormones had legitimate outlets. The penalties for becoming pregnant outside of marriage were stringent to deter people from 'non-legitimate' sex. Efficient contraception has enabled us to have much greater sexual freedom than the generations who went before. Over- rather than under-population is considered a major problem by the West, so society does not pressure us to live such a limited range of lifestyles as earlier generations. We can marry or not marry. We can have children or not have children. We can have relationships with members of the opposite sex or the same sex. We are also bombarded with other choices. Magazines offer sex chat lines so people can phone someone and masturbate to their favorite fantasy. Contact advertisements offer the possibility of getting together in threesomes, swinging with another couple, S&M, 'being a baby' fantasies, bisexual experimentation – you name it. To an extra-terrestrial visitor it might seem as though Western society was sexually uninhibited, but many people are left confused and uncertain about what is ok and what is not. Media norms compete with religious upbringing, people have fantasies that they are afraid to share with their partners, and if what we like is straightforward heterosexual sex within a stable partnership, we can be left feeling boring and vaguely inadequate.

Most adults in the fertile years of life are biologically programmed to want and need sex. This is after all what keeps our species alive. This is good, normal and fun. Generally, society would be better off if people were less obsessed about what other consenting adults do with their bodies. Providing sexuality is not damaging our health, causing unwanted pregnancy, or leading us to neglect our responsibilities, it is generally no one's business but our own. Sexual fantasy and experimentation can be fun. This is not a problem but it can become one if the fantasy overcomes the reality. However, although some sexual fantasies can be fun to act out, it is important to recognize what is behind the fantasies. If you have fantasies about inflicting or receiving humiliation and pain, all may not be well in your shadow world. It might be useful to think about why you have such needs. Where did they arise and what hidden frustrations and past traumas are they expressing? If you have strong masochistic tendencies, either fantasized or expressed, it is unlikely that you value yourself as much as you should. What hidden shame do your fantasies mask? If you like to dominate others, why is this?

Have you had periods in your life when others dominated you? Did this make you angry, frustrated or afraid? Is acting the dominator/dominatrix a way of ensuring that in future you will always be in control? If you need to be 'forced' into sex in S&M fantasies, why are you afraid of admitting that you like and want sex? Were you brought up in an environment where 'nice girls' didn't have sexual feelings where, to go back to the Tony Soprano world, women are virgins and then wives, or whores?

America is supposedly the Western world's most puritanical country – the spirit of the Founding Fathers lives. The majority of the population identify themselves as Christian and many attend Sunday worship. In Britain, a country that to its continental cousins seems puritanical, less than ten per cent of the population attends church services. Yet, in both countries, porn sites are the most frequented web sites on the internet. Policing corporate on-line activity to stop employees spending long hours downloading porn has become a major problem. University computer bills are soaring as students spend hours logging onto porn instead of studying.

Admitting that you really like sex and want lots and lots of it may be much more difficult than acting out a fantasy where you pretend that you don't want it at all. Another important question to ask yourself is whether acting out your fantasies is freeing you from them or feeding them. Are sexual fantasies taking up so much of your leisure time that you are neglecting other aspects of your life? Are sexual fantasies taking over from real sex with your partner? If so, then you can end up in a negative spiral whereby you fantasize and use porn because your real sex life is unfulfilling and your real sex life becomes more unfulfilling because all your sexual energy goes into fantasies.

Anne and Simon's story

Simon and Anne's sex life deteriorated because it took her a long time to have vaginal orgasms. Simon had secret fears about impotence ever since some experiences with girlfriends in his early twenties when, at the end of long evenings out at parties drinking, he had found himself unable to get an erection. Always anxious to keep his erection once he had it, their sex life became a matter of quick intercourse, after which Simon went to sleep and Anne masturbated herself to orgasm while he slept beside her. Anne was miserably unhappy with their sex life, feeling that Simon just wanted to 'shoot his load' and didn't really care about her needs. Frustrated, Anne started to punish Simon. If they argued, and arguments became more frequent, she would refuse to speak to him, sometimes for two or three days at a time, and would sleep in the spare bedroom. There she masturbated and had fantasies with a strong masochistic component – exacerbated by guilt feelings about what she was doing. At the age of six when she became interested in the differences between boys' and girls' anatomy, she had been caught by her mother exploring her genitals with the aid of her fingers and a mirror. Her mother's shock and anger left Anne in no doubt that nice girls definitely didn't touch themselves there!

Anne decided she needed some help with her life direction and where her relationship was going. She attended a weekend workshop of ours where we discussed male and female roles. Anne found that in the anonymity of a weekend group, she could talk to other women about her sexuality in a way that she had never talked to any close friend. The weekend made her realize how valuable her relationship was to her – she really loved her husband – but that she had some deep sexual inhibitions. She also realized that her ways of dealing with arguments – of withdrawing and refusing to discuss the real issues – were a negative

YOUR DARK SIDE

pattern she had learned from her mother. She had absorbed her mother's negative attitudes to sex – women should be passive partners in the sexual act. Anne decided that if she wanted to improve her sex life, she was going to have to take the initiative.

On her way home on the Sunday, Anne went shopping for a bottle of wine and the ingredients for a romantic dinner for two. With the courage of two days' openness behind her, she told Simon what she had found out about herself and told him what she thought his fears were. Anne discovered that Simon's relief in being able to talk openly about their problems was enormous and the dinner ended with some enthusiastic sex on the sofa that reduced them to giggles as it reminded them of their respective adolescent fumblings. They managed a mutual orgasm and Anne began a campaign to brighten up their sex life. She discovered she had an exhibitionist streak and enjoyed flaunting herself in front of Simon in skimpy underwear. Taking a much more active role in their sex life was something she found arousing so that by the time they had sex, she had orgasms more quickly. As their sex life became more varied, Simon found that he could hold erections for much longer periods and his early fears disappeared. Anne had turned the situation round by realizing that it was ok for her to have sexual needs and to do something active about fulfilling them.

⌇⌇

SEX AND RELIGION

Religions have taught a great deal of shame about sex and have at the same time provided havens for sexual abusers. Religion can also be a refuge for those whose early sexual experiences are aversive. If sex becomes associated with harmful experiences, then a life of religious purity can be a way out, a means of escaping the sensate reality of the body and the realm of human emotions.

Sarah's dark side

As a child, Sarah's father adored her – to an extent that she found difficult to handle. He was physically intrusive and when he kissed her he thrust his tongue into her mouth. Her mother watched while this happened and did nothing to prevent it. Even at an early age, Sarah knew this was wrong and spent the rest of her childhood and adolescence trying to keep a physical distance from her father so that he could not touch her. She developed a wide range of outside interests – anything that would keep her out of the house. She joined a church where people spoke in tongues and gave spiritual healing. She found Christianity helpful in defending her psychologically from her father's desires and was determined to remain a virgin until she found exactly the right man.

At eighteen, Sarah won a scholarship and went to a prestigious university in a city far from home; despite parental pressure to live at home and attend a local college. She began attending the university chapel, but found the services boring and impersonal and after a few Sundays did not return. Feeling a void in her life, she noticed an advertisement for meditation classes at a holistic health centre. The classes were Buddhist and Sarah found herself strongly attracted to the emphasis on renunciation. A few months after starting the classes she dropped out of university, went to live at a monastery out of town and began training to become a nun.

Sarah's virginity troubled her. Although she was preparing to dedicate herself to a life of celibacy, she felt that as a virgin she was somehow not a 'real woman'. Sarah had had a boyfriend in her hometown who had been very upset when she had ended the relationship on going to university. She re-contacted her former boyfriend and said she would like to see him. Would he visit her at her university? Pretending that she was still a student and that male overnight guests were not allowed at her women's student residence, she booked them into a motel. They spent a wonderful weekend together, during which she lost her virginity and had enjoyable sex a number of times. Her boyfriend left thinking that the relationship was resumed and that she would be phoning him in a few days. Sarah did not phone. She wrote him a letter saying that she had decided to become a nun and would not see him again. He was distraught and wrote her an angry letter saying she had used him for a 'last fling'. Sarah was shocked at the vehemence but justified it to herself – wasn't that how men treated women? She was glad she had got her own back. She was ordained, took a new name, put the incident out of her mind and spent fifteen years becoming a spiritual teacher in her Buddhist tradition. We will return to Sarah's story later.

ACCEPTING YOUR SEXUAL SELF

Our feelings about sex are closely related to our feelings about our bodies. It is easy for children and adolescents to absorb negative messages about their bodies and sexuality. Sexuality becomes something shameful and forbidden, rather than uninhibited and spontaneous. In our HIV age, we cannot return to a Garden of Eden of sexual freedom. Sexuality today must be accompanied by responsible awareness, but sexuality is still one of the greatest pleasures and joys of human existence. If we are to experience the joy of sexuality and sensuality, we must first come to terms with our bodily erotic selves. This is an exercise to help you contact your early guilt-free self.

≋ **Something to try** ≋

BODY, SEX AND SHADOW – ACCEPTING THE BODY

For this exercise, you need quiet, privacy, warmth and soft lighting. You may want to light a candle and to burn some perfumed oil. The exercise is best done lying down. You could write or type the exercise in large print so that you can refer to the instructions as you go along. Alternatively, you could read the instructions onto a cassette so you can play them back. In this case, leave gaps for visualization between each instruction.

1 Relax and allow tension in your body to seep way.

2 Imagine that you are swimming in warm clear blue sea. Above you, the sun shines in a cloudless blue sky. You are naked and the water caresses your body as you swim through the warm sea.

3 You are swimming towards a silvery white sandy shore. The water becomes shallow and you stand up and wade onto the shore. There are no other footprints here. You are alone and there is nothing to fear.

4 Beneath your bare feet, you feel the hot sand. A gentle breeze caresses your body and the warm sun dries your skin.

5 Beyond the shore, the sand gives way to lush green trees covered in fruit. Through the trees is a sandy path. You follow the path.

Gradually the sand gives way to soft green grass. You feel a soft carpet of cool greenness beneath your feet.

6 You find yourself approaching a temple with yellow sandstone walls. A sweet smell of incense wafts out through the open doors.

7 You enter the temple, naked and unafraid. In the center of the temple is an altar on which is a brazier in which burns a vigil fire. A green altar cloth with embroidered flowers, trees and birds covers the altar. On the wall behind the altar is a stained-glass window with a beautiful face in the center like that of an angel with flaming red hair. All is light, warm and joyful.

8 You stand in front of the altar and commune with the vigil fire. The flames leap higher as though to greet you. A vision appears in the flames of the interior of another temple in a warm country long ago. There, white-robed priestesses and priests came to tend the temple fire, but here there is only you. You are sad that so few come to tend the flame, for you sense that each of us has need of this vigil fire.

9 Then you sense in the temple the presence of the Divine. You stand before the Divine naked and unashamed. Divine love flows over you, bathing your body in golden light, loving all of you – body, soul, mind and spirit. You are a vessel of the Divine Spirit that watches over all. You sense that there is no shame in loving desire and no shame in the sexual love of another; for all love is a reflection of the love that the Divine has for us. You commune with this feeling for a while – a feeling of total acceptance of all that you are – beneath the loving gaze of the Divine Father and Mother of all.

10 After a while, you feel it is time to depart. You follow the grassy path back through the trees. The grass gives way to sand and emerges on the sandy beach. You wade into the blue sea and when it is deep enough you begin to swim. You turn on your back and float in the warm and welcoming sea. You float until you find yourself dreaming once more of your everyday room in your everyday world. You sense it is time to return.

11 You open your eyes and you are back in your room once more. You are alone, at peace, and with a memory of love and acceptance for your body and yourself.

Whenever you are faced with doubts about your body or feelings of self-loathing, you can repeat this exercise to remind you that your animal self is a gift and it is worthy of love, respect and care.

Spontaneity and playfulness are important in sexual love. In sex, do you make the first move, or must your partner always approach you? Do you do fun sensual activities together, like massage, taking a bath or shower together, going away for a weekend and spending a long time in bed? Do you show you care? Do you tell your partner that you love him or her? Do you buy him or her surprise presents and remember the occasions when you should buy a present? Do you do things for your partner without being asked? Touching, telling and giving are all ways of showing our feelings for one another. Touch gives us the reassurance that our bodies are acceptable to others. Sensual experience and physical intimacy with a loving partner create and fortify us for the reality outside. A truly loving sexual relationship can bring the joy of being loved and accepted in our entirety.

FIVE THINGS TO REMEMBER

1 Your body is on loan and won't be yours forever. Look after it well. Pamper your body with massage, steam baths and exercise, and enjoy making it look its best. Your body will appreciate it.

2 If people tell you that your hang-ups about your body are mistaken – believe them. They can you see objectively, you can't.

3 If you are habitually tired or depressed, your body may be the cause and not your mental state. Check out your diet and exercise routine before rushing to try prescription drugs.

4 Don't become angry with your partner because you are ashamed to admit your sexual needs. If you don't discuss your needs but are secretly punishing your partner because you feel unfulfilled then you are damaging both of you.

5 Some sexual fantasies are fun and can enhance your sex life, but others reflect deep-seated psychological problems. If your fantasies are about abusive situations, think about doing things to increase your self-esteem so you need neither abuse nor be abused.

7

Your dark side
at work

The dark side affects relationships not only in our personal and family lives but also in the workplace. Most of us work in organizations of some kind or another. How we interact with those organizations and the people within them will be influenced by our early experiences of being the newcomer to an organization. The first organization that most of us join is school. We may or may not look forward to this new adventure. Often we will have been prepared for 'big school' by nursery. If we have older brothers and sisters, we will have heard lots about it and going to school will be a rite of passage that puts us on equal par with our older siblings. If we are firstborn or only children, then we will be pioneers. If we are outgoing adventurous children, we will be excited by the idea. It will be a chance to make new friends. If we are timid children who feel overwhelmed in crowds and hate doing new things, then the idea may be hell. This first experience will affect how we join organizations for the rest of our lives. If we found it intimidating, the pattern is likely to repeat itself. If we found school friendly and welcoming, we will carry this expectation with us. Like most expectations, they are more likely to be confirmed than disconfirmed. Cementing an attitude or set of expectations is far easier than overturning them. If we expect people to like us and to treat us well, these are the signals that we fire off and people will usually take us at our own estimation.

How well do you cope with new situations? When you enter a new organization or situation, do you feel that everyone else has had an extra lesson that you haven't had? Everyone else seems to understand the situation and you don't. Rationally you know that you are starting on an equal basis with everyone else. No one has had preferential treatment; but this strange unsettling feeling persists. Most of us, especially as children, find it vitally important to fit in, to be accepted. We do this usually by emulating those around us. We camouflage our real selves and adopt the cloak of peer-group conformity. Unconsciously we learn that in order to be accepted we have to dissemble. We cannot expose our real selves. This can be repeated throughout life so the person we truly are becomes ever more stifled and suppressed. Apart from feeding our shadow side, this may prevent us realizing our full potential. We may never reveal our true selves – good or bad – but be always acting a part. This makes us self-conscious. In every new situation and encounter, instead of re-acting to the needs of the situation, our energies are channeled into evaluating what is going on. 'Am I like these people? Will I fit in? Will I have to adapt to protect myself?' And yes, while you are wasting time doing all this, the others will get a step ahead.

⪡ Something to try ⪢
EARLY MEMORIES OF ORGANIZATIONS

Our first organizational experiences influence how we will react to joining new organizations. This is an exercise to help you think about your early organizational memories.

1 Imagine yourself back in your childhood. It is your first day at school. You are at home about to set off. What was the atmosphere – were your parents happy for you, worried, sad, not there at all to support you? Were you happy, tense or fearful as you set off?

2 What happened when you arrived for your first day? Did all go well, or were there any unpleasant experiences such as being ridiculed, ignored, bullied, getting lost, losing something, not finding your way to the bathroom in time?

3 Now think about your adult life. When you enter new jobs or social groups, do you take any expectations with you? Do you find it easy or difficult to fit into new groups? How does that impact on your social life, whether you join clubs and associations, whether you change your job when you should?

⪡⪢

WORK AND SELF

Many of us define ourselves in terms of what we do. We are telesales people, marketing vice presidents, nurses, website designers, waiters. Our job title defines our status, income and lifestyle. If we have a job that engages and fulfils us, that is fine. If work is simply a means to earn a living, then we may find that our jobs suppress aspects of ourselves that we would like to develop and develop aspects of ourselves that we do not like at all. The wrong kind of work, which might be the right type of work for someone else, can leave us alienated and unfulfilled.

Tom's story

After graduating from university, Tom was offered a job with a prestigious accountancy partnership. Neither of his parents had attended university and they made considerable sacrifices to finance his university education. They were delighted that their struggle had been worthwhile. Tom passed all his professional examinations at first attempt and came high in national listings. By age 25, he had a good income and by 29 he owned an apartment in the center of the city that he had bought outright from bonuses. He also had an expensive car, clothes and sporting equipment, and he had paid off all the loans that his parents had taken out on his behalf. Everything was going brilliantly and Tom was being tipped for a partnership.

To celebrate his 30th birthday, Tom took two weeks' holiday and went trekking in Peru to visit a sacred city that he had read about as a boy. In the mountains, he had a profound spiritual experience that he could not name, but which was somehow deeply meaningful. On his first morning back at work, he started to feel dizzy and collapsed. He was rushed to hospital where doctors concluded that he had suffered a mild heart attack, probably precipitated by a delayed reaction to the high altitudes in Peru. A period of convalescence followed, during which Tom continued to work using his laptop and mobile. Three weeks later, he returned to the office. He had been there an hour when he collapsed again. He was hospitalized again. The doctors could find nothing wrong with him, but kept him for a week in order to carry out blood and other tests – none of which showed anything abnormal.

On the day before he was due to be discharged, a nurse asked Tom if he was looking forward to going back to work. To his horror, he was filled with a sensation of overwhelming and terrible grief. He burst into tears and then began to sob that no, he wasn't looking forward to returning to work. He hated his job. The nurse called for the assistance of a hospital psychiatrist who spent an hour talking to Tom and realized that he was on the verge of a major crisis. He referred Tom as an outpatient to a psychotherapist. His repressed self had broken free. We'll tell you more about Tom later.

Career choice can be surprisingly haphazard. Some of us have burning career ambitions from an early age. We know that we want to be actors, doctors, religious professionals, airline pilots, or whatever, and we focus our education towards achieving our ambitions. However, most people leave school or university with qualifications that are general rather than specific. The career path we take will depend on the available jobs at the time and we may find ourselves taking a career direction that is nothing like anything we might have imagined. Once we have started on a particular track, it can be hard to change. Promotions and better job offers come more easily within a job sector you know something about rather than starting anew in a different field. The longer we stay in a career, the more difficult it can be to break out. Our career is defining our direction rather than us directing our career.

For many people this sort of compromise is good enough. It's not perfect but we can live with it. However, some people find that to survive in their jobs they need to become something they are not.

They have to act a role, do unpleasant things, make harsh decisions following corporate rules and strictures rather than the dictates of their own feelings and moral values, or they may simply find themselves in jobs that require them to be extroverts when they are really introverts – and vice versa.

More about Vivianne

I never thought of myself as a raving extrovert until I started training as a psychologist, when I suddenly found myself the most extrovert person in the class. In fact, I'm only mildly extrovert, but psychologists tend to be introverts. Suddenly I found myself in the situation that the extreme extrovert knows well, but if you are an extreme extrovert, it won't bother you. You probably won't even notice. As a moderate extrovert, I did notice. My laughter was too loud. I wanted to chat at what turned out to be inappropriate times. Things that seemed hilariously funny to me didn't seem so to my colleagues. I asked too many questions and had to be careful not to talk too much in seminars. And sometimes I felt like a large friendly dog that finds itself in a room filled with furniture. It was hard to avoid knocking things over. I found myself having to curb the way that I behaved. A brief post-qualifying period working with psychologist colleagues at a psychiatric rehabilitation unit was hell. With the patients everything was great, but I was just too bouncy for my colleagues. The solution came when I entered private practice. I found I attracted extrovert clients, ran workshops with other extroverts and became a lecturer.

DARK SIDE AT WORK

Are you the same person at work as you are at home – and if not, why not? The mouse at the office can be the monster at home, who takes out the difficulties, stresses and humiliations of work on partner and family. Dominated by a forceful partner at home or just hassled to death with squalor, squabbling children, money worries and cramped living conditions, the cowed spirit at home can get his or her own back at the office and become the tyrant ruling a fiefdom with a rod of iron. Work can be the perfect place for the negative dark side to flourish. Bosses can let the dark side of leadership take over so they become workplace bullies. Others will play dark side games with you.

Do you ever feel crowded by someone at work? He or she is too close. It is as if this person has taken over some of your space and is giving you no room to breathe or function as you wish. You feel stifled in his or her presence so that your main objective in any encounter is to escape as soon as possible, to breathe your own air. Your instinctual energy goes into fight or flight mode. Your rational mind is fighting to preserve an air of normality but you know that something strange is going on. This person is leaking dark side. This can be unconscious – the person is oblivious to their effect on others – or it can be deliberate, a strategy to get what he or she wants. In business, it may work; reinforcing the negative pattern and making a vice appear a virtue.

Rod's dark side

At the suggestion of his employer, Rod came to see me (Chris) for career coaching. It was clear he resented it. He was the managing director of a small but profitable subsidiary and couldn't understand why he had been singled out. His part of the business was doing well, comparatively better than other subsidiaries. However, the parent corporation was concerned that none of Rod's senior management team stayed very long and they would never give any clear reasons for their departure. Rod too seemed genuinely bewildered as to why this was so. He saw himself as a natural leader who commanded considerable loyalty. Everything would seem to be fine until suddenly his managers upped and left.

Rod's manner provided the clue. He was tall and heavily built, though fit looking. He strode into the room, saw two low chairs around a coffee table, selected the chair that was usually mine and sat down. As soon as I sat down, he lent across the coffee table and told me he couldn't understand why he was there and made some disparaging comments about the parent corporation's board. Rod occupied my room as if it was his own and started to use his physical bulk to coerce me into agreeing with him. He lent forward and loomed over me like an incoherent grizzly bear. I let him talk himself to a standstill and then asked him to enact a recent meeting with one of his staff. After considerable reluctance, he got going. When he was in full flow, I asked him to describe the size of the person he was talking to. He indicated with his hand. The person was four foot high.

Later I got him to talk about his childhood and had a sudden insight. 'Do you look like your father?' I asked. Rod blinked. Yes, he did. Locked in his dark side was a behavioral template of how to exercise authority – his father's. As a young boy, Rod had hated the demeaning way his overbearing father had treated him, but unconsciously he absorbed the message that this was how to get your own way – and he had copied it ever since. The next sessions were spent teaching Rod that he didn't have to feel threatened by people: there are others ways of managing people than cutting them down to size.

⧖

BEING IN CONTROL

If as children we are victims of abusive power and control relation-ships, our ideas about power and authority will be distorted. To pro-tect ourselves, we may seek in adult life to be the person in control. At work, we get ourselves into a superior position by striving to be at the top of our chosen tree. From that position, we can ensure our own safety, by suppressing or intimidating anyone who might be threatening. Another strategy is avoidance. Unconsciously, we never again want to be in that pattern. We want neither to control nor to be controlled.

Alan's dark side

Throughout his childhood, Alan felt over-controlled by his dominating mother. As his parents' only child, he received mixed messages. His mother adored him, she told him, and therefore wanted to run his life for him, because she knew what was best. Alan's father seemed an ineffectual onlooker to Alan's upbringing. At school, Alan reacted by rebelling. He was frequently in trouble and left school and home as soon as he could. Alan never lasted in a job for longer than a year and all his jobs were 'Mc-jobs'. This was fine at 19, but not so good at 29.

Alan was a conscientious worker and did well in his tasks, which were well below his capabilities. After a while, he was invariably offered promotions. As soon as he was offered a promotion, Alan left. If he took on responsibilities, he would have to commit himself to the organization. People would be controlling his life and he would be controlling other people's. Alan hated telling other people what to do.

It was surprising that someone so independent could cope with being in a bottom-grade job, but he found it fine. Alan wasn't really there. In routine jobs, he just switched off. His body might be doing what his boss told him, but his mind was somewhere completely different. In fact, Alan had a rich fantasy life and could so compartmentalize his thinking that he could run a sword and sorcery epic in his head with himself as hero while serving burgers.

At the age of 28, Alan became engaged. His fiancée was more educated, with a well-paid job. In some ways she reminded him of his mother, but rather than controlling him she encouraged him to believe in himself and his abilities. He decided to enroll in night school classes in web design. Alan found web design fascinating. Previously his creativity had been channeled into fantasy. Now it was being channeled into the outer world. When his training finished, with his fiancée's backing, Alan left his job and set up as a freelance web designer. For some people, working on their own and not being part of an organization is lonely and demotivating, but Alan loves it. It gives him the control over his life he always craved. Alan's business is becoming a success.

WORKPLACE BULLIES

Authoritarian organizations such as the armed forces and the prison service attract people who are comfortable in hierarchical situations where lines of power and control are firmly delineated. These organizations and others with an authoritarian management style can attract people who need to mask their underlying sense of anxiety by dominating others. They may think of themselves as natural leaders, when in reality they are insecure bullies. Bullying, whether in the workplace or elsewhere, is a regression to childhood behaviors that have not been outgrown. The ranting boss who makes impossible demands and sets impossible deadlines is a toddler seeking instant gratification. It is back to the three-year old's, 'Gimme! Gimme!' as it is wheeled around the supermarket in the shopping cart, driving parent and everyone else in earshot to distraction.

Bullies function by subordinating others and undermining their sense of self-belief. To do this, they have an unerring instinct for detecting those who have shaky self-belief. If you find yourself constantly in situations where you are being bullied at work, you need to think about where the abusive pattern started. Go back to your childhood. Are you repeating a pattern of appeasing or not standing up to a dominating parent, older sibling, school bully or teacher?

Bullying bosses undermine our confidence and self-esteem by constant criticism and impossible demands. If we work for a bully, we will start to think that our work is below standard. Unless we watch out this can become a self-fulfilling prophecy; as confidence falls, so do our standards. If this is happening to you, you either have to complain to senior management or get out.

Wendy's dark side

Wendy is a talented copywriter who worked for a small company owned by a self-made millionaire on the fringes of the music business. Wendy's boss was a workaholic who demanded that his staff work long hours – which Wendy did. The boss demanded that people work on Saturdays – which Wendy did. Staff had to attend company functions and entertain clients over the weekend – which Wendy did. With each new demand, Wendy responded as she thought a positive career-minded employee should. She was rewarded with constant faultfinding and when she asked for a pay rise, she was told that a monkey could do her job. Thoroughly demoralized, she decided to get out. She prepared a portfolio of samples of her work and went to two interviews hesitantly, by now thoroughly convinced that her work was useless. The first company interviewer told her that the portfolio was the best he had seen. The second company interviewer asked if she could stay for an hour to have a second interview with the company chairman straight away. She was offered a job on the spot. A week later, offer letter in hand, she gave her old boss one-week's notice. On the Friday, she left him a present on his desk, her replacement and its week's wages – a small furry toy monkey and a packet of peanuts. Sometimes letting the shadow out to play can be fun.

≈ Something to try ≈
MORE ABOUT SHADOW

In the exercise at the end of Chapter 1, you started to identify what you dislike in yourself and in others. This is an exercise to help you identify some more attributes of your shadow.

1　Here is a list of negative qualities. Take a sheet of paper and try going through the list word by word, saying each word in the list aloud.

aggressive	egocentric	pompous
arrogant	egotistical	possessive
bitch	envious	pretentious
boring	greedy	racist
bossy	hypocritical	rude
brooding	immature	ruthless
cold	inflexible	sadistic
condescending	insensitive	secretive
controlling	irresponsible	stupid
cowardly	jealous	superficial
critical	judgmental	thoughtless
cruel	lazy	vain
defensive	manipulative	vindictive
dependent	masochistic	violent
devious	neurotic	whiner
dishonest	obsessive	wimp
domineering	passive aggressive	workaholic

2　Now imagine someone calling you that word and say it aloud again.

3　Notice your reactions. If you would be hurt or upset if someone called you that word, write it down on your sheet of paper and put a tick beside it.

4 Now think about the word. Has anyone ever called you that world in real life – adult life, teenage years, or in your childhood? If someone has really called you that word and you felt upset about it, make a second tick against it.

5 Go through the word list to see how many 'trigger words' there are here for you.

THROUGH A GLASS DARKLY

6 Now take things one stage further. If you can remember someone telling you that you were any of these things, try to remember when and why. Was the accusation just? We remember things because they offer new information, or information that does not easily integrate with other information that we hold in memory. If certain words jump out for you, why is this? Is it because you were accused of them unjustly? Is it because the accusation hit home? Or are you secretly afraid that the word might apply to you?

7 If more than one person has accused you of the same failing and you don't agree, they could be wrong, but think about it. If people are getting you wrong, why is this? Is there something you are doing that contributes to their mistaken impression of you, and can you change this?

By completing this exercise, you have started to confront your dark side – well done! Many people never do this at all.

People use these exercises in different ways – and not always how we would expect. A banker client did this exercise and decided that 'aggressive, arrogant, ruthless bastard' applied to him. He likes the phrase so much that he's put it on his screen saver at work, followed by – 'and those are my good points.' In the competitive environment in which he works, he knows that at times he needs a hard and aggressive edge to clinch the deal. Acknowledging that this harder side is there gives him the confidence he needs when the going gets tough. And at night when he switches off his computer, he knows it's time to switch off his aggressive self to live out his other life. He doesn't need to take his aggression home.

FIVE THINGS TO REMEMBER

1 Are you an organization person – and what kind of organization? If you feel lost in large organizations, you may blossom in a small one. If you need a lot of personal freedom, you might need to work for yourself.

2 Some people play power games at work. If you are working for a bully, speak up or move out. Bullies damage our souls.

3 'Ruthless self' might be an essential part of your survival skills in some jobs, but it is only a tool to be picked up and put down. Remember to leave ruthless self behind when you go home.

4 If your work is turning you into someone whom you don't like very much, change your job.

5 If you are taking days off sick, are you ill, or are you unhappy at work? We spend 75,000 hours or more of our lives at work. Do

you want to spend this amount of time at a job you dislike? If you are unhappy at work, change your job. If your job is making you ill – change your job.

8

Money and
your dark side

*I've been rich and I've been poor.
Believe me, rich is better!*

Mae West

The dark side evolves throughout life, building on and feeding off the dark side created in childhood. The dark side feeds on insecurity and for some people insecurity is so strong that they spend their lives trying to feel safe. Unfortunately, life is not a safe business, so trying to feel secure is a never-ending battle. For many people, security is bound up with income. Attitudes to money can have an important impact on the dark side of our personalities. Our attitudes to money are far from rational. They are based on an unconscious evaluation of what we should have, what we feel we deserve. One person's poor can be another person's rich. What one person considers just enough to live on might be impossible riches for someone else. We are conditioned by our expectations. These expectations will be influenced by the expectations of partners, parents or peer groups. Sometimes the expectations are in touch with reality; sometimes they are too high or too low.

As well as unconscious expectations, we also constantly compare ourselves with friends, colleagues and acquaintances. How much are they earning? Am I keeping up? We compare how we are doing in relation to everyone else. There is nothing wrong in this. Taking stock from time to time to see where we are going and what we are achieving is an invaluable tool. The dark side is when this becomes obsessive; when we put all our energy into keeping ahead of everyone else. We become obsessed by materialism. We start to define our identity by what we have rather than what we are. The dark side encourages conspicuous consumption as a sign of victory and success, rather than because we want or need the products we buy for ourselves. The dark side makes us glad we have something because it makes other people jealous, rather than because we value it for itself.

Dark side envy and anxiety can make money a source of never-ending dissatisfaction. We can be eaten away by money issues so that whatever we have is not enough. Something positive, 'I want to do as well as I can for my family and myself. I want to get as far as I can in this world,' is warped and twisted into a negative goad that tears away inside us. Nothing we have is good enough; whatever we earn or are given is unappreciated because the focus has already moved on to the next thing. As soon as we acquire something, we cease to see its value. We are back in the nursery where another child's toy always seems infinitely preferable to our own. Swap the toys around and we still feel the same. Instead of a healthy competitiveness that leads to rewards, we are in a negative world of jealousy, envy and dissatisfaction. Money is good, but Gordon Gekko's 1980s mantra of 'Greed is good' is not. Greed is an attempt to fill a void inside – some people overeat, some people compulsively seek sex, and others overspend. None of these things will fill a void that is emotional and spiritual.

The old truism that money does not buy happiness is true. Neither spending nor accumulating money will make us happy if the rest of our life is unfulfilled. Many of us, especially women, will know the mad frenzy that can take over in clothes stores, especially in sales. We feel we have to buy something because it's so cheap. We have to have it. A friend's mother was a compulsive shopper. When she died recently of cancer, she had two full length walk in closets full of clothes bought in sales. Sometimes she even bought three blouses all the same in different colours because she wanted them all. She could not make a choice about what to have and what not to have. Some of the clothes had never been worn. Many had been worn only once. It was a sad legacy of an unhappy woman whose life was never fully lived.

Just as a life dedicated to shopping is unlikely to fill us with joy, so a life spent in the pursuit of money for its own sake is likely to be a miserable one. The Greek myth of King Midas tells how the fabulously wealthy king of Phrygia, in what is now modern-day Turkey, was offered a gift by the god Dionysus. Midas asked for a gift without thinking through the implications. He asked Dionysus to grant him the gift of being able to turn everything he touched into gold. Midas, in his greed, forgot to insert any exclusion clauses. In the end, he could touch nothing. Even his own daughter was turned into gold. What Midas had most desired became a curse. The ancient Greeks were good at their parables.

Unless we are aspiring saints or would-be Buddhas who want to leave the Wheel of Rebirth, poverty is not going to make us happy either. Many people have real money worries, but worrying about money can also be a substitute for dealing with emotional insecurity. This is a short quiz about money to see if money worries are troubling you.

≋ Something to try ≋
MONEY AND YOU

Circle one only.

1 Has your income fallen substantially during the past year?
   a. No, not at all
   b. No, not a great deal
   c. Yes, somewhat
   d. Yes, a great deal

2 Most of my friends have:
   a. About as much money as I do
   b. Less money than I do
   c. Slightly more money than I do
   d. Much more money than I do

3 Compared to my parents, my standard of living is:
   a. Much better than theirs
   b. Better than theirs
   c. About the same
   d. Worse than theirs

4 Relative to your present income, how deeply in debt are you?
a. Very little or not at all
b. I only have debts I can afford
c. Enough to feel uncomfortable
d. Way over my head

5 There always seem to be things I want that I can't have.
a. Strongly disagree
b. Disagree
c. Agree
d. Strongly agree

6 Circle as many as apply. I am worried at present about:
Not having enough money
Having insufficient health insurance
Not advancing in my career
Not having savings for the future
Job insecurity
Unemployment
Not being able to pay children's university fees

7 Circle as many as apply. Which of the following have bothered you in the past year?
Constant worry and anxiety
Fatigue
Loneliness
Feeling worthless
Headaches
Insomnia
Feeling guilty

Weight problems
Lack of interest in sex
Feelings of despair

In questions 1–5, score 1 for each a, 2 for each b, 3 for each c and 4 for each d. For questions 6 and 7, score 1 point for each circled answer. The maximum score is 37. If you score 25 or more, you are likely to have serious money worries. If you score under 10 you are very much at ease with money matters. Between 10 and 24 you are like most of us; managing. It's not easy is it?

In the swiftly changing economic climate that we live in today, concerns about money may be realistic, but they may not be as realistic as we think. Our grandparents' generation had much less money than most of us do now, but people probably worry as much or even more about money than their forbears. Money represents all sorts of psychological qualities for us. It represents the ability to obtain essential items, but also power, prestige and choice. Money represents security. When we have money in the bank, we can feel safe. However, stock markets fluctuate, pension plans may or may not pay as much as we hoped. Some of this we can try to offset by sensible financial planning, but other events are due to global factors that are beyond our control. There are also more important things to worry about. Health is more important than money; though many people severely abuse their health by overworking and leading destructive lifestyles that damage their family relationships in order to earn money they may never be fit enough to enjoy. Being overly concerned about money can make us selfish and miserly. However little we have, someone else has less and would benefit from even minor generosity. Paradoxically, giving away small amounts of money will help us get money into perspective and to value it for what it can do for others as well as for our immediate families and ourselves. Giving a small portion of our incomes away will make us feel more secure. We are in control and inputting into life instead of life being in control of us.

Charitable giving is a wonderful playground for our dark side. The dark side performs charitable works. It does so on the same principle as much corporate giving. It is a way of advertising our ego images and of showing what nice altruistic people we are. This does not mean that we have to give this up. Most good causes derive their support from sponsors who recognize consciously or unconsciously that they are reaping reciprocal rewards from the relationship. It is important to be honest with ourselves about our reasons for ostentatious giving. Any kind of giving to good causes is worthwhile doing, but we must not deceive ourselves about our motives and what we are looking for in return.

True altruism is not ostentatious. It means doing something for others without expectation of direct reward. Of course, we do get rewards from giving, because we do not do things unless we get some kind of positive feedback. That feedback might be the pleasure of seeing another's smile, the knowledge that we are contributing something to alleviate world poverty; or the satisfaction that we have given something back to the world.

☙ Something to try ☙
SECRET GIVING

Practice secret giving. Of course, secret giving is not completely altruistic. You will derive satisfaction from it, but there is an interesting message in this secret giving which your unconscious may appreciate. Normally, we advertise our good actions and hide our unworthy ones. Try keeping a bit of the goodness of yourself back and be more open about the badness. This helps us achieve a balance and people will respond to you differently if they sense you are a whole person.

Tell no one, except perhaps your partner, but on a regular basis give something, however small, to a worthy cause.

As one car sticker says, 'Perform random acts of senseless kindness.' Spontaneity is fun.

MONEY AS POWER

Some people are unable to be generous with money and use their wealth to get people to do want they want them to do. Money can also be used within families to convey love, withdraw love, and to manipulate.

Philip's story

Philip's father was a millionaire. From a blue-collar background, he started life as an engineer, began an engineering contracting company, became involved in the North Sea oil boom at just the right time, and by the age of 50 owned a multinational company. Philip was his father's only son and it was his father's ambition that eventually Philip should run the business.

From his schooldays, Philip had to work all his vacations in the business. Philip's own ambition was to be a doctor. He applied and was accepted for a place at a prestigious medical school. Then the family rows began. Philip's father would not finance his son at medical school. He was to enter the business and work for his living. Philip refused but found himself with a medical place but no money. He started the course and worked five nights a week in a factory to pay his way, but he became exhausted. He began to fall behind with his studies and failed his first-year examinations. Philip gave up and felt a complete failure. For three years, he dropped out, taking a series of dead-end jobs and having no contact with his family. In the meantime, his parents divorced. One evening, his father turned up at his apartment with a box of groceries as a peace offering. He persuaded Philip to come home and work in the business.

Philip worked in the business for ten years, but the relationship with his father was difficult. As his experience grew, Philip wanted more authority and autonomy but his father could not let go of the reins. The years passed and his father showed no signs of retiring.

When he was 63, Philip's father took a holiday in the Caribbean where he met a woman who was recently divorced. They started a relationship and three months later they were married. Twelve months later Philip's father had a heart attack and died. He had made no will and Philip found that the business belonged to his stepmother, who promptly sold it, giving nothing to Philip or his two sisters.

Philip had spent all his adult life in the expectation of inheriting the business and with it considerable wealth. Now he had neither job nor money. He had wasted his life in a job he hated and in being subordinate to his father. He was unable to cope with the blow and began drinking heavily. He obtained a job in a firm in the same industry as his father's but lost it after six months due to absenteeism. The drinking became heavier still. Philip was plagued with constant self-recriminations and could not get over the feeling that he had wasted his life. He was overcome with bitter self-hatred. He felt he had trusted in his father and that his father had betrayed him.

Philip's father had used money to pressurize his son into a life that he did not want and Philip did not have the inner strength to resist. Family money can be used as a bargaining chip to manipulate people into doing what we want. Rich parents can ruin their children's lives by keeping them on a leash waiting to inherit family money. Some of the greatest and most destructive family rows are caused by wills, or the lack of them.

Money is as much an issue in poor families as in rich ones. Parents may encourage all manner of undesirable behaviors through money. We need to be clear on what we are rewarding.

Jim's story

Jim is from a poor area of Glasgow who learned aggression from the age of eight when some other boys in his neighborhood beat him up. When he went home crying, his father beat him again – for losing. In order to win his father's approval he had to become rougher and tougher than the other boys. Every time he got into a fight and won, his father gave him extra pocket money. Jim's father used money to teach his son that violence pays. Jim's father prepared Jim for the life of a criminal and that is what he became – but more about that later.

Rewarding children with money when they succeed in school examinations or sports can condition them to believe that they are only valued when they win something. Rewarding effort is good, but children need to know they will be loved and valued if they fail and will be given support to try again. Parents who have not received this type of support themselves may not know how to give it. It can also be difficult for parents to make the leap of imagination required to see that their children's needs are different from their own. What seems 'fair' to one person in terms of financial support may not seem so to another.

Peter's story

Peter's parents have no formal educational qualifications. They had both worked hard all their lives and though their wages were low, they saved hard and bought a small apartment. Peter was their only son and he was an excellent scholar. His school was in a poor neighborhood with high truancy levels and drugs and violence problems. Peter refused to get involved but studied. His best subjects were history and languages – not subjects that seemed to lead to any kind of career. Peter's father was proud of his son's school success when he was younger but as Peter progressed through school with no definite ideas about what he wanted to do afterwards, Peter's father grew increasingly worried.

Peter's father began to resent the time his son spent on reading books. He started to comment that when he was fifteen he was already working and contributing to support his family. Peter took the hint and during his summer vacation he got a job at a local store, working six days a week. When he returned to school, the store manager offered Peter part-time work for as many hours as he wanted. Peter took up the offer and agreed to work three evenings and a Saturday. As the demands of school increased, Peter found the store hours too much. He told his father that he was going to work in future on Saturdays only but his father flew into a rage and insisted that Peter kept working as before. In fact, he thought Peter should leave school and work full-time at the store where there were good prospects of becoming a supervisor or manager.

Peter was horrified and said no more about reducing his hours of work. He carried on but his schoolwork suffered and his teachers concluded that he was not motivated enough. Peter's father was constantly asking him what he was going to do when he left school and Peter plucked up the courage to say that he wanted to go to university. Peter's father told him that the idea was ridiculous, especially when Peter said that he wanted to study history. Parental pressure won and Peter left school and became a trainee manager at the store.

Peter did well in the store's management program, but internally Peter was in turmoil. He found his job excruciatingly boring. He started having nightmares. Sometimes he was smashing up the shop and terrorizing the customers with an axe. Other times he was shut in a coffin and couldn't get out. He became seriously worried about his psychological state. He began to feel that he was heading for some kind of nervous breakdown but felt unable to confide in anyone. Instead, he went to the public library and took out some psychology books to find out if he was going mad. Peter knew nothing about psychology and found the books fascinating. Peter suddenly knew what he wanted to do with his life – he wanted to be a psychologist.

Now Peter had a goal, the dreams stopped. He worked as much overtime as he could for a year in order to save as much money as possible. He applied for and was accepted for a place on a psychology degree. To Peter's surprise, this time his father was supportive of his idea. Being a psychologist was a career job and his father could understand what he wanted from study. However, his father didn't offer any financial help and Peter didn't want to jeopardize the improved relationship with his father by asking. Part of him bitterly resented the fact that his parents didn't help him, but he also loved his father and saw that his father couldn't help the way he was. Peter decided he was going to have to earn his way through university – but he could make it.

FIVE THINGS TO REMEMBER

1 Don't be mean with money. If your partner is a spendthrift with a compulsive desire to run up credit card bills, then you need to do some hard negotiating and persuade your partner to cut his or her credit limits. If you are complaining that your partner buys things for him- or herself, then you need to discuss how you allocate money. How much should be for joint expenses, future retirement saving, emergency reserves, and how much should you each spend on yourselves and one another? Talking honestly about money is the way grown-ups behave. Be a grown-up.

2 Don't play games with inherited money. Decide what is fair to partners and children, make your will and stick by it.

3 Think about your attitudes to money. If your parents did not treat you generously with regard to money and emotional support, are you repeating negative patterns in your own relationships?

4 Give some money away – and don't tell other people. Small amounts are fine. For many good causes, they can make all the difference.

5 It's fun to be generous. Be generous.

9)
Dark side
and depression

Our dark side is about parts of ourselves that we have repressed. Repressed self is closely linked to depressed self. Depression can result from bad situations in which we are trapped and which we are powerless to change. This can happen at an early age if we have abusive parenting or are bullied at school. We learn survival strategies to deal with the abuse that work at the time, but can be counter-productive in adult life. We may begin to believe that we deserve to be treated like this; that it is normal. In fact, if parents whom we love are the abusers, believing that we deserve the abuse can be less threatening to our sense of self-esteem than admitting that our parents are severely dysfunctional people who do not give a damn about us. If we are unloved, we are at risk of being abandoned. The nightmare scenario of every young child is abandonment. This is why children found Walt Disney's film *Bambi*, in which the young deer loses its mother to hunters, to be extremely frightening. Better to believe that our parents do care about us really and we are provoking them in some way than the frightening truth. We convince ourselves that we just have to grit our teeth and bear it. In later life, we may tolerate abusive relationships at home or work because that is how we expect life to be. As children, we cannot change the situation we are in. As adults, we can.

⊱⊰

CAUSES OF DEPRESSION

Depression can be caused by physiological imbalances in brain chemistry. Our neurophysiology is faulty and this can only be rectified by external means such as mood-enhancing drugs. However, many people suffer in the short or long term from depression caused by a distorted view of the world. Some people are inclined to believe that everything that happens to them must be their responsibility. This can be good and bad. It can leave us feeling empowered – if what happens is down to us, we have the power to change it. If we believe we have no control over what happens to us we become passive, accepting, and are unable to run our lives. Believing that some of what happens to us is our responsibility is a healthy belief. However, if we are depressed we tend to selectively filter the facts. We forget the good things that happen to us – which must surely be our responsibility as well – and we remember only the bad things. Everything is our fault, we do everything wrong, we are useless.

⩔⩔ Something to try ⩔⩔
GIVING THE RIGHT EXPLANATIONS
FOR THE BAD TIMES

This is an exercise to help you notice how you explain events in your life.

1 Think of four positive things that have happened to you in your life. It might be passing an examination or a driving test, a particular relationship, having a child, or getting a particular job.

2 Next, think of four negative things that have happened to you, such as divorce, failing an examination, losing a friendship through a quarrel, an illness.

3 Now visualize each event. Take them alternately, a positive event and then a negative event and so on.

4 With each event, write down its main causes: was it due to your own effort or actions or lack of them? Was it due to chance or luck? Did someone else take the initiative and make the event happen?

5 Now look at the pattern of your attributions. Do you process information about events in a biased way? Is everything always down to luck, chance or the intervention of someone else? Conversely, is everything always down to you? Or are only some things down to you – either all the bad things or all the good things? If all the bad things are your fault and the good ones are down to chance or someone else, ask yourself – is this really likely? Are you just putting yourself down? On the other hand,

if all the bad things that have happened to you are someone else's fault and everything good is your responsibility, ask yourself if this is true? It may be that it is, but it is important to check that you are not engaging in shadow avoidance here. Is there anything that you could have done to avoid getting into or to lessen the impact of the negative situation in which you found yourself? Are there signals that you can recognize for the future that can help prevent these bad things happening to you again?

HELPLESS AND HOPELESS

Negative thinking tells us biased and inaccurate information, so that if we are depressed we think: a) the cause is internal – 'It's my fault'; b) the cause is stable – 'Things will always be like this, they can't change'; and c) the cause is global – 'This affects everything.' And down we go in a spiral to d) 'This happened to me therefore I must be a bad and worthless person.' If nothing bad ever happens to us – if we never fail an exam, have an automobile accident, or lose a lover – then our negative thinking style may not cause us too many problems. In fact, some people spend the whole of their lives trying not to let anything bad happen to them. They drive safely, stay in unsatisfactory relationships, only try to get qualifications that are below their optimum level of competence, and take jobs that do not stretch them. Fear of failure protects them against the future – for long periods. However, life is full of challenges and disappointments. Loved partners die, parents become ill and need full-time care, accidents happen, our secure jobs disappear due to corporate restructuring. Life is not a safe business. When someone with a negative thinking style does experience a major disappointment, he or she may not be able to deal with it. The next step is depression.

Some people seek to protect themselves from negative events at all costs. Other people are so afraid of bad things happening that they unconsciously invite them. Negative thinkers expect bad things to happen to them. This can become a self-fulfilling prophecy. If you expect never to succeed at a job interview, every aspect of your verbal behaviour and body language will mark you as a loser, and your prophecy will be fulfilled – you will not get the job.

For many people, depression can be avoided by avoiding negative thinking, learning to deal with or avoid high stress, or doing things to increase our self-esteem. What we become depressed about will depend on our personalities. For competitive people with high status needs, losing a job or failing a driving test can precipitate depression. For people for whom relationships are the most important thing in life, failure of a relationship will be a precipitating cause. Thinking negatively about the past or future can precipitate depression. If we are afraid of things that might go wrong in the future, then each new day is a potential ordeal. If we spend our time in 'if only' regrets, then each new day is wasted in fruitless thinking about the past. Depression about lack of achievement is not related to objective reality. Leonardo da Vinci, painter, sculptor and mechanical genius, thought that he had frittered away his talents and had never amounted to much. Over 500 years later, people flock to see his works and some of his paintings, such as the Mona Lisa and The Last Supper, are among the most famous in the world. Faulty perception is the problem here and even a genius like Leonardo could suffer from being overly self-critical and seeing what he had not done rather than what he had achieved. Even a Leonardo can be too focused on 'what might have been'.

How can we overcome the negative thinking that leads to depression? First, we need to recognize and diagnose the problem. We need to think about the good things that have happened to us. We have to focus on what we have achieved and what we are going to achieve, rather than on what we have not done in the past. We have to recognize that bad things do happen to good people. Life is full of unexpected and random events. It's 'just the ways things are'. Some psychologists believe that depression results from an illusion of control. Baby Boomers were the post-Second-World-War generation who were taught that they could have it all. Women were told they could be 'Superwomen': they could have beautiful homes, loving partners, spotlessly clean, well-educated and beautiful children, and a successful full-time career. Some people do manage all these things, but for most people life is more mixed. We succeed in some ways but not in others, we get part of the package but not all of it. Things go wrong – and this is normal. Unlike their parents and grandparents, the Baby Boomer generation was not taught that life is a risky business with ups and downs. As a result, Baby Boomers suffer from high rates of depression. The world did not meet their expectations. The world is not always generous or fair. Sometimes bad things happen and we just have to work our way through them. We have to remember that this is worth doing. The gift of consciousness is an extraordinary one. Being alive is the best thing of all and life is worth holding on to.

⊰⊱ Something to try ⊰⊱
REMEMBERING THE GOOD TIMES

If you do suffer from depressive thinking, it is important that you remind yourself that life does not have to be like this. This is an exercise to help you think of a non-depressed past, present and future.

1 Take some sheets of paper and a pen with brightly coloured ink – turquoise, pink, orange or red.

2 Head one sheet 'Past'.

3 Excluding your current life situation, write down five good things that have happened to you in the course of your life so far, preferably from different periods in your life.

4 Now think about three good things in your current life. Remember, however bad things may be in your life, there is always one good thing – you are alive. To be a sentient being in this extraordinarily beautiful cosmos is an amazing thing.

5 Now think of three simple things that you would like to do over the next month and how you could set about doing them.

6 Once you have done the first three things on your list, do the exercise again, remembering to do the preliminary stages of thinking about positive events in your life as well. Remembering the positive reminds you of what you can do. It sets the scene for creating more experiences that are positive.

DARK SIDE AND CHOICE

When we are depressed, the dark side can be a heavy weight that tells us we are no good, that we can never achieve anything, that our life situation is unalterable and intolerable. We can find that we have unconsciously absorbed a whole series of negative messages about ourselves that can seem impossible to shift. This isn't true. Fortunately, personal change is much more possible than we usually think because we all have the gift of will. Sometimes, this is well developed and sometimes it is not, but one of humankind's abilities is to be able to decide to do something and do it. We all have the ability to choose to exercise free will – even in extreme circumstances. Psychiatrist Viktor Frankl was imprisoned in concentration camps during the Second World War after he turned down the opportunity to flee his native Austria because he could not desert his extended family and patients. What impressed Dr Frankl most of all was that despite the terrible conditions under which people lived – the deprivation, starvation, cruelty, and the constant fear of death – they could still make choices between right and wrong, good and evil. They could choose to help another prisoner or ignore his or her plight. They could choose heroism or cowardice, unselfishness or ruthless self-interest. They could believe or not believe, hope or despair. Similarly, we all have choices in our lives – and the right to exercise them.

This is an exercise to imagine how things can be different. Remember that visualization is a very powerful technique. By visualizing how we would like things to be we can create the right conditions for change. Allow your imagination out to play.

What if you were not depressed? How could you think differently?

1 If you are currently depressed, think about how things might be if you were not depressed. What would happen to you if you were not depressed? What would people notice about you?

2 Now choose three things that you would change about yourself or your environment if you were not depressed. Think about smaller things rather than bigger. Maybe you would change your hair color, clean up your apartment, change your car, book a weekend away, go for a walk in the park, or telephone a friend.

3 Even though you are depressed, do these things anyway. Doing the first thing will be the hardest. Depression creates inertia, so don't spend too long thinking about it – just do it.

Mood affects behavior and behavior affects mood. If we do things we want to do, even if we do not feel like doing them (if you can cope with all the contradictions in this sentence), then our mood will change. Not doing the things we feel we want to do makes us feel more depressed. Doing things empowers us and shows us that it is possible to do more.

⩥⩤

IF ONLY

In the Norse sacred texts the *Eddas*, Doubt is called the River Ifing.

*Doubt is the name of the river that flows
between the worlds of the gods and the giants;
it shall flow freely unfrozen forever;
no ice ever forms on Ifing.*

Eddas: Vaftrudnismál, v16

Ifing is the if only syndrome. Even in the Scandinavian northern wastes, no ice will ever form on that river, so the giants cannot cross it. They will never become gods. The *Eddas* had some sound ideas about anxiety too. The Vikings were a practical people.

*A fool lies awake at night
turning things over in his mind;
at daybreak he is exhausted,
and all is the same as before.*

Hávamál, v23

Many people suffer from the if only disease. 'If only I hadn't had that last drink, the accident wouldn't have happened.' 'If only I hadn't said that cruel thing, my father wouldn't have died thinking that I hated him.' We run scenarios through our heads imagining how things might have been if we had performed just a single small action differently. Sometimes we imagine that things might have turned out worse than they did. A study of Olympic medal winners showed that bronze medalists were much more satisfied with the outcome than those who had won silver. Why were people happier with the lesser prize? Silver medalists were tormented by the idea that if only they had tried just a little bit harder, if only something hadn't gone slightly wrong, they would have been standing on the topmost podium. Bronze medalists were relieved to be there at all. They could all too easily have been among the 'also rans'.

When something bad happens our brains try to find a cause. If we suffer from negative thinking, we will tend to create reasons that reflect negatively on us. Say, for instance, that you are involved in a car accident. You may decide it was or was not your fault; it could or could not have been prevented.

Responsibility attribution	Internal	External
At fault	I did it and it was my fault.	Someone else did it and it was his or her fault.
No fault	I did it but it was not my fault.	Someone else did it but it was no one's fault.

Here are some examples of how accidents happen. Let's assume that your car is dented, but no one is hurt.

Responsibility attribution	Internal (my fault)	External (someone else's fault)
At fault	1 You are driving too fast and crash into someone.	3 Someone is driving too fast and crashes into you.
No fault	2 You are driving and are distracted because your child has an asthma attack. You crash into someone.	4 Someone's tyre blows out and his or her car crashes into you.

If you are processing information rationally, you will decide that some of these situations were your fault and you could have done something to prevent them. If you suffer from the 'if only' disease, you will believe that you could have prevented all of these situations occurring, 'If only I had done something different'.

Rather than saying 'if only', take a deep breath when something goes wrong and say, 'Everything that happens to me is a learning experience.' We start then to focus on the future and not the past. So, what can we learn if events happen to us like those described above?

Responsibility attribution	Internal (my fault)	External (someone else's fault)
At fault	1 You are driving too fast and crash into someone.	3 Someone is driving too fast and crashes into you.
	Positive response: *I did a bad thing and I am suffering for it. In future, I need to drive more safely. In future, I will drive more safely.*	**Positive response**: *Sometimes accidents happen. I won't let this put me off driving, but I'll make sure I'm alert when I'm at the wheel.*
	Negative response: *If only I hadn't done it. I'm a bad and stupid person to drive so badly. I deserve to be punished.*	**Negative response**: *If only I had gone to to work a different way. If only I hadn't stopped to buy a newspaper, I wouldn't have been there at that moment. If only...*

No fault	2 You are driving and are distracted because your child has an asthma attack. You crash into someone.	4 Someone's tyre blows out and his or her car crashes into you.

Positive response:
My response as a mother was a natural and instinctive one and couldn't be helped, but if an emergency occurs in the car in future, I will focus on my driving and pull over before reacting.

Positive response:
Sometimes accidents happen. I won't let this put me off driving. I will make sure I have my tyres checked regularly.

Negative response:
If only I hadn't reached over to my child. If only I hadn't brought my child with me. If only...'

Negative response:
If only I had gone to work a different way. If only, I hadn't stopped to buy a newspaper, I wouldn't have been there at that moment. If only...

Are you getting bored yet with 'if only'? If you are an 'if only' person, say to yourself:

'If only' people are boring people. I am not a boring person.
I am a person who learns from mistakes.

The next time you catch yourself sliding down the slippery slope towards 'if only', go and stand in front of the bathroom mirror and say:

'If only' people are very, very boring people. Something bad
has happened. What can I learn that will help me in the future?

Talking to your reflection in the bathroom mirror may seem a silly thing to do. It may even make you laugh – and laughter is a healing process. However silly externalizing your thoughts may seem, it is a lot less silly than the nonsense we tell ourselves inside our heads. When we have to take our thought processes out into the external world and look at them, we test them against reality. What can seem huge problems and issues when we go over them in our minds seem quite different in the greater scheme of things in the external world.

Going over a scenario to imagine how it might have been different is known as counter-factual thinking. When people think about better alternatives to the real outcome, they feel bad about themselves. This type of thinking can easily turn to anger – an anger that turns inward on oneself. This type of anger is extremely stressful and can lead to depression. A negative spiral begins. We got something wrong, we did not do ourselves justice, so we are worthless and incompetent. Sometimes when people think like this it is due to scripts learned from parents at an early age. People brought up in a blame culture learn to blame themselves when things go wrong. Taking responsibility for things going wrong – thinking that it would have been a good idea to have revised for the exam a bit harder, to have read more about the company before going for the job interview – can be useful if we are oriented towards the future. If we are present and future-oriented, we can learn from our mistakes. If we are focused on the past, counter-factual thinking can be a form of self-abuse.

ON NOT BEING PERFECT

I used to be Snow White, but I drifted.

Mae West

Being realistic about others and ourselves is the most important aspect of dealing with the shadow. Realism helps us steer a course between cynicism, which makes life boring and dull, and romanticism, where we are out of touch with reality. We find a balance between ego inflation – we think we are much better than we are and ignore the shadow – and ego deflation – we think we are much worse than we are, shadow overwhelms us, and we are constantly depressed by our own unworthiness, uselessness, incompetence and inability to cope. The Middle Way is to recognize that we are good and bad, weak and strong. Sometimes we get things right. Sometimes we get things wrong. We make mistakes, but we also have inspired moments where we get things exactly right. This is normal, this is human, and we are both normal and human – and so are most other people. Here the mirror trick can be useful again. If you make a mistake, go to your bathroom mirror and say to your reflection:

'I am not perfect, but I am ok'.

If something did not go as well as it should, this is a learning opportunity and a challenge to try to change similar future situations. Everyone goes through the phases when nothing seems to go right. Successful people are those who are undaunted when they get things wrong. Your mistakes can help make you more successful. This is an exercise to help you think about your mistakes.

⋙ Something to try ⋙
LEARNING FROM MISTAKES

Here are some ways of thinking about your mistakes.

1. If you are unhappy with something you have done or not done, it is important to take it out of the internal world of your head where you can waste lots of time telling yourself what a bad or useless person you are. Instead, take a sheet of paper and write down what happened. Then write down what you could have done to avoid the outcome that displeased you.

2. Then write down something like, 'The next time I have an important meeting at work, I will get up an hour earlier than normal and I will set off to work early so I do not feel rushed and stressed when I arrive', or 'The next time I go out for a drink, I will not get drunk. I will have three alcoholic drinks and then change to fruit juice or water.'

3. This is one way of bringing a change in behavior into the real world. Another way is to say it aloud. Try reading out loud what you have written.

4. A third way is to tell someone else. Many people are brought up to believe that to admit any failing is a sign of weakness. We desperately hide our failings behind the mask of the persona. A mask is exactly that – a mask. A mask is not a real person. Real people, strong people, experiment with life. When we experiment, we find that some things do not work and we make mistakes. Learning to be open about our mistakes is a sign of a strong person not a weak one. This is one reason why erring

politicians now specialize in televized admissions of wrongdoing. 'Owning up' to our mistakes and weaknesses can make people perceive us as courageous and strong.

5 If telling someone else what you have done and what you intend to do about it is too dreadful to contemplate, try telling yourself out loud in a different way – record what you have written on a tape and play it back to yourself. If you get used to hearing yourself admit that you cannot do everything perfectly then it will become easier to admit this to other people.

Admission is a way of bringing shadow out of the deepest, darkest, most secret place of ourselves and into dappled sunlight, somewhere we can see the shadow as it shrinks in the bright sunlight to something more manageable in size.

FIVE THINGS TO REMEMBER

1 Not everything is your fault. Life is a mixture of what we do, what others do and what happens by chance. If bad things happen to you, you are not a bad person. If bad things happen to other people, they are not bad people.

2 When you are depressed, you still have the power of choice. Do some very small thing to make your life a little better – and keep on doing very small things – just one at a time will do. After a while, your life will be better.

3 'If only' is a waste of time and 'if only' people are very, very boring. Do not be boring.

4 You are not perfect, but you are OK.

5 We all make mistakes. Some people are clever people who learn from their mistakes. You are a person who learns from your mistakes.

10)

Dark side
and anger

The shadow self is often an angry self. If we repress anger and do not acknowledge it, it will spill out. Sometimes the result is acts of violence – physical or verbal. Sometimes the shadow is a lot sneakier. We find all manner of devious and malicious ways to attack by stealth the person who has offended us. Owning anger is difficult for many people, but owning anger does not mean we have to have a blazing row with someone. It may mean that we need to look coolly and rationally at what has upset us and to decide if we need to do something about it. Anger that is allowed to build up has negative consequences both physically and emotionally. It causes us stress and, ultimately, repressed anger can lead to all sorts of illnesses.

WOMEN AND ANGER

Suppressed anger causes us emotional distress because we feel disempowered – we do not believe we have the right to feel angry. This problem can be particularly acute for women, who traditionally have been given less freedom to express anger than men. Women often feel much more responsible for the atmosphere in any social unit they are in – whether work, family, or one-to-one relationship. They do not want to 'rock the boat' or 'spoil things'. It is easier all round to let things slide, push things under the carpet, grin and bear it. Women have been taught to please, soothe and conciliate. Some of this training is helpful when dealing with screaming toddlers. In situations where people are mistreating us, then not to express anger may just allow someone's negative behavior to be perpetuated. Sometimes this can be from a real fear of male anger or violence. People who have been brought up in homes with violent fathers may have to repress their own anger for fear of violence against them. Men brought up in such an atmosphere may unconsciously decide as small boys that they will never behave like that. When they do become angry in a relationship, they may suppress it out of fear of what will happen if anger is 'let out'. Others unconsciously repeat negative patterns they have seen in their families.

Linda's story

Linda was raised in a large family with a violent father. Her mother was a practicing Catholic who believed it was women's lot to put up with whatever their husbands did. Linda left home early to live with her boyfriend whom she'd met at school. Rob came from a family with a dominating mother who nagged him constantly. Linda discovered that Rob expected her to organize all their finances and pay all the bills. He had no concept of cash management and spent all his spare money on clothes and CDs. Rob also expected Linda to make all their decisions – where they would live, what they did every evening, what they ate. Rob never took the initiate and never made a suggestion about anything. This was the complete opposite to what Linda was used to. In her family, her father had made all the decisions and consulted her mother about nothing. In some ways, Linda felt like a middle-aged mother with a teenage son. In other ways, she felt more like her father.

Linda became increasingly angry at the situation but could not articulate what was wrong. Her family never discussed emotions. In fact, they never discussed anything much at all. Too many subjects, such as her father's violence towards her mother, were taboo. Linda found that she was becoming aggressive with customers in the restaurant where she worked and that she was provoking arguments with Rob over the most trivial things. She hated the way she sounded when they argued but couldn't stop herself from shouting at him. Their rows became more frequent and verbally violent. One day Linda threw a mug at Rob that missed him but smashed against the kitchen wall leaving a hole in the plaster. Linda was horrified and realized what she was trying to do – to provoke Rob into hitting her to prove that he was a man after all. She stopped the argument at once and realized that she didn't like the person she was becoming.

A few weeks after the mug throwing, Linda overheard some of her work colleagues talking about an apartment they were thinking of renting together. Without pausing to think, Linda found herself asking if she could be included. It was only a few days later when she gave her colleagues her share of the deposit and the first month's rent that she realized she was really going to do it. She was going to leave Rob. After-wards Linda was ashamed of the cowardly way she left Rob, but she had no family experience of explaining how she felt and didn't know how to tell him she was leaving. Instead, she went home early from work at a time when she knew he would be out and moved out. She left him a note and an envelope with enough cash to cover her share of the bills for the next month, but she did not give him her new address and telephone number. When she left her apartment keys on the kitchen table and shut the door for the last time, she felt a huge sense of relief. She didn't much like the way she was leaving Rob, but she knew that the person she would become if she stayed was a lot more damaging.

By a curious and dysfunctional quirk of the human psyche, it is eas-ier to react to or suppress our anger than to deal with the cause of it. A negative way of dealing with anger is to slam down the phone, kick the cat, or to throw a file at the office wall. A mature way of dealing with anger is to say, 'I don't feel that I am being treated cor-rectly.' 'When you do that it makes me feel you are not considering my feelings.' A positive way of dealing with anger is to communicate about the issue that is making you angry. A negative way of dealing with anger is to behave in an angry manner. If we feel stronger than or equally strong physically or emotionally to someone who has made us angry, we may act with spontaneous aggression and ver-bally or physically attack him or her. If we feel frightened by some-one or by the consequences of retaliation, then we may still attack them, but passive–aggressively. We may engage in malicious gossip and back stabbing to 'get our own back'. We may 'wind people up' about the person who has offended us and feed a sustained campaign against them. There are myriad devious ways we can deal with our anger, all of which are much more negative and self-destructive than simply walking up to someone and saying, 'It made be really angry when you did that.'

In order to be honest about anger, we have to feel empowered. We have to feel we are worthwhile people who deserve to be treated with respect. If we have low self-esteem, we will not be sure of that fact and we will allow people to mistreat us. Allowing people to mistreat us doesn't mean we will feel happy about it. It simply means that we will feel angry, frustrated and vengeful. If we feel disempowered, we may respond to feeling angry by a show of withdrawal. We stomp off in high dudgeon. We slam doors, lock ourselves in the bathroom in floods of tears and refuse to come out. We go out for a long drive in the car and refuse to speak to our partner on our return. We put on our stereo headphones and refuse to talk. In other words, we withdraw our engagement with the other individual with the intention of making him or her plead to get it back. If this works, then it can make us feel temporarily powerful, but we are sending others and ourselves confusing signals. We are signaling that we are not adults and cannot behave like adults. We are prima donnas to be placated and gods to be appeased.

⇌

SEEING RED, RIGHT AND WRONG

Anger distorts our perceptions. We talk about 'seeing red'. It is as though everything we think, feel and see is colored by the anger. We are likely to make errors of judgment when we are in this emotional state. We are likely to think that we are absolutely right and the other person is absolutely wrong. This is rarely, if ever, true. Anger focuses our attention so that everything seems simple and extreme; we cannot see the complexities. Biologically, anger is a precursor to fighting. For fighting, we need to concentrate on the situation in front of us. These physiological reactions are helpful if we are about to be physically attacked. Most of the time they are redundant and just serve to cloud our thinking. When we are angry, we find it difficult to see clearly the motives of others. We will think that people's actions that have angered us are deliberately malicious. This may be true, but usually people make us angry through actions that are selfish, thoughtless and careless, rather than deliberately malicious. A negative way of dealing with anger is to plot revenge. Revenge can result in hours expended on elaborate sadistic fantasies. The more disempowered we feel in real life to confront the person who has angered us, the more elaborate the revenge fantasies will be.

For those who have little access to power or authority, expressing aggression can be a way of alleviating the tensions they feel about their low social status. A woman may constantly belittle her partner for his lack of achievement, status, and failure to provide her with a good standard of living. Even if both partners work, in a social environment where a woman has been conditioned to expect that a man will 'provide' for her and that her male partner will have a higher status job than herself, it is the man who may bear the brunt of her anger if the couple's lifestyle does not meet her expectations. In a verbal exchange, a man can more easily rely on his stronger voice to shout his partner down. If he feels physically violent, he may channel the violence into thumping on a table but aggression can escalate to physical violence.

Aggressive adolescents who feel they have little stake in the society around them can alleviate their frustrations by forming street gangs and fighting with young people of similar age and status. They may also turn to vandalism. People who have never been vandals themselves (except perhaps when a public payphone refuses to work or a slot machine swallows our money and does not deliver the promised chocolate bar or parking receipt) may talk of 'mindless violence', which suggests that vandalism is purposeless. Humans do engage in purposeless activity, but not that often. We do things because we gain something from them. Vandalism for the disempowered can be a way of being in control. We can demonstrate our contempt for state authorities by destroying street signs and subway carriages. We can demonstrate our frustration with a consumer society in which we are valued by ownership of consumer goods that we have no legitimate means of obtaining by smashing store windows. Vandalism is often tied in with graffiti. Gangs may vandalize a neighborhood and then put their territorial markings on the area in language which other gangs but not ordinary passers-by will understand. The markings signal, 'these streets are ours – beware.'

We learn aggression first from our parents and then from siblings and peers. Punitive parents and teachers who beat children teach them that aggression is the normal behavior for dominant adults. Some family cultures actively encourage boys in particular to 'act like a man,' 'not to be a softie,' to defend themselves and 'give more than they got' if attacked. Children are quick to learn. If they are encouraged or allowed to be aggressive they will realize that they can get things they want from aggression – and the pattern is set.

More of Jim's story

Remember Jim from Glasgow, whose story we told in chapter 8? In his teens, Jim became a member of one of Glasgow's notorious gangs and began a career in crime. In his mid-twenties, he was sentenced to life imprisonment for killing a rival gang member with an axe. His first few years in prison were hell – for himself and for everyone else. He was constantly being deprived of his prison privileges for acts of violence. After fifteen years, he was enrolled on a prison education program. He started to study sociology and psychology and began to understand the reasons for his violence. At the age of 45, he decided to turn his life around. I (Vivianne) first met Jim when he was enrolled on a pre-release program. He realized that he resorted to violence because he'd been conditioned to nothing else, but also because he wasn't articulate. If he was taunted or anything went wrong in his life, he knew only one way to express his displeasure – with his fists or with the nearest available weapon. 'It's all right for you,' he once told me. 'If someone says something to you that you don't like you know how to use words to respond. I didn't.' The education program taught him about words and words gave Jim a new source of power. He had one burning ambition – to use the newfound power to work with young people from his neighborhood and to deter them from making the same mistakes as he did.

Violence occurs when people's sense of self-esteem is threatened. Mocking someone or calling them names can erupt into violence. Violence can also be triggered from invading someone else's space.

Road rage often begins from traffic frustrations. These are everyday life events. They are impersonal in the sense that they are no one's fault. Maybe someone does something that infringes on our territory – our lane, our opportunity to pull out to cross a busy junction, a parking space we have spotted. We make a gesture, exchange some aggressive words, and things begin to escalate. Street violence and road rage often begin from verbal exchanges. The person who thinks he is losing the argument reacts violently and a fight begins.

Abuse in families is often triggered by frustration at outside events. Abuse increases when people lose their jobs or are under threat of job loss. Alcohol is a major factor in aggression and violence. When we are drunk, we are more emotionally reactive. We are more likely to react violently if someone angers or threatens us. We are more likely to become angry because our tolerance of frustration decreases under alcohol. When drunk, we lose our sense of empathy with others. We are less aware that we are inflicting physical pain or emotional hurt and will go way beyond any limits that we normally set ourselves. Some depressant drugs used to treat anxiety, such as diazepam, have a similar effect to alcohol.

Factors in the environment may increase aggression beyond the normal boundaries. More aggressive crimes, such as murders, rapes, family violence and assault are committed in hot weather. As temperature increases, our bodies become physically aroused and our heart rates rise. This in turn makes us more aggressive. If there is an angry confrontation between two people on a very hot day, it is more likely to end in physical violence than on a cold day. We literally become 'hot and bothered'. Road rage too increases when temperatures go up.

AGGRESSION AND SEXUALITY

Crimes like rape are often thought to be due to sexual arousal. It is true that sexual arousal can be involved, but rape is about aggression. Rape is a crime in which there is a victim and a perpetrator and the aim of the perpetrator is as much to hurt and humiliate the victim as to alleviate sexual frustration. There are periodic debates as to whether pornography feeds the shadow side of our personalities. Does pornography cause us damage? Studies show that erotica causes sexual arousal but it is not associated with aggression. Pornography that features sadism, violence, bestiality and cruelty is different. It stirs up a dangerous combination of sexual arousal and aggression. Men who have seen violent pornographic films are more likely to fantasize about committing rape and are more likely to think that they might rape. People who perpetuate physical and sexual abuse are often childhood victims of abuse. People who have been in abusive situations where they had no power to do anything about it can be left with high levels of free-floating aggression. What they are angry about will stem from anger at aspects of their childhood or frustration with their daily lives. Rather than admit the real problems, people can displace this anger in all sorts of negative ways. We may decide that everything that is wrong with society is due to white people, black people, rich international bankers, the media, women, or whatever. Some people release their frustrations through crime.

Others may seek to justify their aggression by harnessing it in the ostensible benefit of a worthy cause. The cause may be ethical in itself – animal rights, GM food protests, or affirmative action – but protest movements of all kinds suffer from the problem of hangers-on who are using the movement as a vehicle for expressing their own frustrations. They turn peaceful demonstrations into riots and hijack the concerns of responsible citizens as an excuse for fighting the police and smashing store windows. They undermine the movements they pretend to serve. One of the problems of anger is the heady wine of self-righteousness, which allows us to justify all kinds of vicious behavior. Anger can be an infection that takes over the psyche and obliterates reason. This doesn't mean that we shouldn't become angry about social injustice. A negative outlet for that anger and frustration is to attack the perpetrators. A positive outlet is to do something, however small, to change the situation and to raise people's awareness that something is wrong.

⩥⩣

ANGER AND WILL

Anger is strongly associated with the energy of will. Will is the energy that gives us 'get up and go'. It impels us to action – even when things are difficult. We do not have to be angry in order to have a strong will, but strong-willed people have large reserves of energy that they tap and utilize. When outlets of that energy are unavailable or thwarted, then the energy can become negative anger. The more fulfilled we feel, the less thwarted and angry we are. Instead, we have will. Like anger, will focuses our attention, but it is an attention unclouded by emotion. This is a useful quality in business life and in many other environments. Running a successful business requires a clear focus, goals and purpose. The qualities required in the competitive business world overlap with those of hunter and warrior. Those who run governments need the same mindset – one that sees beyond the difficulties and is not daunted.

We experience will instead of anger when we feel in control of our lives. This is one of the qualities of a mature adult personality. Many people do not feel in control of their lives and it is true that we can never be completely in control. In fact, being completely in control would be very boring indeed. Nothing unexpected, random or exciting would ever happen to us. Everything would be exactly as we planned, expected and imagined, and our world would be bound by the limits of our individual imaginations. Unexpectedness adds a new zest and opens us to experiences we would never have thought of having. We all know 'control freaks' who try to be 'on top of everything,' and to 'have everything at their fingertips.' Such people are a nightmare to work with. They cannot delegate and will not allow others the same autonomy they demand for themselves. To attempt to control everything and everyone leads us to become control freaks. To attempt to control nothing is to fail in our adult duty of taking responsibility for ourselves. Between the competing energies of control and lack of control, we must find a point of balance.

Aerobic exercise can help give us energy and clarity of thought. So, too, can visualization techniques. Visual imagery has an enormous and under-estimated power on our psyches. If we visualize positive things happening to us, this will affect our unconscious expectations and the signals we put out to other people. If we are in a positive frame of mind, people respond to us differently than they would if we were signaling negativity and defeat. When used to treat illness and disease such techniques form part of the science of psychoneuroimmunology – the power of the mind over the body.

⩗⩘ Something to try ⩗⩘
ENERGIZING YOURSELF

This is an exercise to help you access the energy of your will.

1 Sit with your spine straight and allow your breathing to become slow and steady.

2 Once you are relaxed, visualize a column of white light pouring down over the crown of your head. The white light enters the crown of your head and flows through you. It flows down through your skull, cleansing your psyche. It flows right through your body and down into the floor beneath.

3 With the flow of the white light, all negative energy is removed from you. You feel a clear, light energy filling you and uniting you with the spiritual realm.

4 The light continues to flow down through you and over you. It is a continuous white stream without beginning and without ending. The streaming light clears out all negative thought. It clears out jealousy and anger. It clears out all barriers that prevent you realizing your inner powers. It leaves you focused in the present, with a strong desire to order your life in the way in which you wish.

5 Now say to yourself:
I have the power to change what seems changeless;
I am an Energizer in the world;
I have the will to change the pattern of my existence,
with love and passion, I can harness that will;
deep within me are reserves of strength, energy and power.

6 Allow the light that you are visualizing to cease flowing. The clear sense of purpose that contact with the light has given you remains. You find that you are in your own space, with a focused energy and purpose that you can use whenever you wish.

7 Repeat this exercise whenever you need to have focused energy.

Energy and anger are strongly related. When we carry blocked anger in our psyches, we will have energy blockages. Buried anger is like toxic waste. It poisons everything that surrounds it. Releasing the blockages can transmute anger into energy and courage. By developing energy and courage to overcome obstacles that challenge us, we develop and grow. Will is particularly important in the psychologies of Dr Alfred Adler, founder of the social psychiatry movement, and Dr Roberto Assagioli, founder of psychosynthesis, a psychotherapy that recognizes that we all have a spiritual centre. Energy combined with will becomes 'Will to Act'. It is the power to overcome inertia. Energy and conviction help us strive to build a better society. Will to Act gives us the will to achieve our true aims. By developing our wills, we can transmute aggression and anger and regenerate the personality.

≶ **Something to try** ≶
TRANSFORMING ANGER

Anger is a fiery emotion that makes us cold to others. Anger is also an energetic activity. Sometimes that activity is expressed outwardly, exploding into violence. Sometimes it is contained inwardly and we seethe with anger like a bubbling cauldron, or we become inwardly cold, like ice. This is an exercise to explore how you experience anger.

1 Think about how you express aggression.
   Do you express it?
   Do you erupt into violent words or actions like a fiery volcano?
   Alternatively, do you become cold, brooding and vengeful, like an ocean before a storm?
   Do you repress your anger, rather than expressing it?
   Do you deny your anger; pretending that you never experience it at all?

2 Recall the last two occasions on which you became angry. What caused your anger? Maybe there are particular situations that make you angry:
   driving in heavy traffic (road rage)?
   crowded places (territorial anger)?
   people who pressurize you to impossible deadlines at work (anger of disempowerment)?
   situations where people are being oppressed or abused (righteous wrath)?
   situations where you feel demeaned or humiliated (threats to your self-esteem)?

3 One way of dealing with anger is to turn it into something else. Expressing ourselves can be a channel for releasing the energy bound up with anger. Here are some ideas.
   Turn your energy into creativity. Paint a picture, write a story or poem, or write in your diary. Remember that artists are often easily frustrated people who are subject to rages. The anger of

frustration will be released if you give it an outlet through which to express itself.

Donate your energy to a cause. Righteous wrath can be an extremely negative emotion if it remains simply that. If we direct the energy that makes us angry about a situation of injustice or abuse into a worthwhile activity such as joining and working for an organization to help change the situation, then our anger can become a source for good. Many idealists and freedom fighters have been inspired by anger against a system of injustice.

Anger causes energy blockages that have to be cleared. You can channel anger into doing something about your environment. When you become angry, try tidying, clearing out and cleaning your living space or your office. Prune all those overgrown bushes at the back of your house. Re-ordering your environment in a more satisfactory way will give you a sense of control and will be a useful outlet for your energy. You start to manifest your will.

Go for a run or work out in the gym. 'Pumping iron' takes up energy and makes us feel better about ourselves. When our self-esteem is high, we feel less threatened by other people and we can get the behavior that made us angry into perspective.

☆

FIVE THINGS TO REMEMBER

1 It is normal to get angry.

2 People who claim they never get angry are deceiving themselves.

3 Disempowered anger is a disease that makes us ill. It can also make us dangerous. If you are angry, tell people why. Tell people, don't shout.

4 Anger is an energy. It can be transformed into energy to act.

5 When you are angry, do something positive and useful.

11) Realizing your potential

Within us all is a potential self, the life unlived. It is how we could have been if circumstances had been different. Within the potential self is all the vast and limitless potentiality of the human race – whatever can be or has been thought, attempted or achieved. The potential self can be a vehicle for good, a powerhouse for change and improvement. Tapping into the collective unconscious, the group mind of humankind, and drawing on the richness and profusion of its ideas, we can transform our view of the world and our part in it. Potential self is the key to our true personalities.

However well meaning our families, family pressures and expectations can mean that children grow up differently from how they might have been. It is rather like a young seedling not having the right water, soil and light. We can become misshapen or distorted from our real and true essence. 'What might have been' does not go away and is not lost. It lies dormant as part of potential self. Some of the qualities that we have never been allowed to express are socially undesirable. Others may have been considered undesirable in the mini-society of our own families, but perfectly acceptable in someone else's. Celtic noble families used to foster out their teenage children to other families of similar standing. They enjoyed the pleasures of childhood and then sent them to work through their adolescent traumas in someone else's household – someone who was much less emotionally involved and had less stake in the way they might turn out. In this way, young Celtic nobles could find their own identities.

You may have potential aspects of yourself within you. How can you tell? Do you find yourself giving people advice on how to live their lives? Do you tell friends that it would be a great idea to give up their well-paid jobs to set up an organic farm? Have they ever thought of downsizing, embracing a more rural lifestyle, traveling around the world? Are you always telling others that they should get fit and start going to the gym? If so, do you go to the gym? Or are you offering the advice that you know you should take yourself.

More about Tom

We left Tom after his outburst about his work as an accountant led to him being referred to a psychotherapist. Tom felt that the therapy sessions could help him, but in the macho atmosphere of Tom's firm, he couldn't admit that he needed to see a therapist, so he lied and told his boss that he had to attend a prolonged course of physiotherapy. He arranged to see a therapist at the end of her daily schedule, which meant that two afternoons a week, Tom left work early. Instead of working his usual 60 hours a week, this cut his working week down to around 50 hours. Tom immediately felt less stressed, but his therapy sessions showed that the outburst in the hospital room had been true – he hated accountancy.

The therapist referred Tom to a careers coach who gave Tom a battery of psychometric tests. These confirmed what Tom already knew – that he had no interest in accountancy – and showed that his strengths were people skills and his interests were in the arts. Tom's favorite subject at school had been art, but he was realistic enough to know that this could be a much loved hobby but he didn't have the talent to be an artist.

Tom decided to plot his escape from accountancy. He reawakened his interest in the arts and subscribed to the friends' and membership programs of the leading museums in his city. He read their magazines and began to take an interest in the latest trends, personalities in the art world, auction prices and museum news. He visited new exhibitions and attended fund-raising events and gala dinners. He began to know who was who. After six months, Tom saw exactly what he had been looking for – a job as a Financial Director of a museum that was working on a plan for a new gallery complex dedicated to modern art. Tom lacked the wide range of experience of some of the other candidates, but his obvious enthusiasm, and interest in and knowledge of the art world got him the job.

Tom is taking a keen interest in the training and development of his immediate subordinate – something she is very pleased about. His plan is to train her up so that after a year, he can delegate most of the routine financial management. He is developing his role to take a major part in fund-raising and investment management. Tom's working week is back to 60 hours, but many of those hours are spent at fund-raising events and exhibition previews, which he enjoys. The illness of eighteen months before is something Tom values because it gave him the permission he needed to let go of a job that was not 'him'. If he hadn't been ill, he might never have made the shift. He believes the illness was entirely psychosomatic.

IN YOUR DREAMS

We can discover a great deal about the hidden aspects of ourselves from dreams. To analyze your dreams, look for recurring patterns and themes. Dream symbols are individual. They will mean one thing in the context of one person's life, relationships and personality, and something quite different to someone else. Not all dreams will be significant, but we can usually sense when a dream is trying to tell us something important, even if the content seems at first baffling or bizarre.

The shadow appears often in dreams. Have you ever had a dream of being chased by a monster, supernatural being, or something so frightful that you dare not turn round to see what it is? This is a classic shadow dream. Something in our psyche scares us and is trying to make itself known. These dreams can be terrifying, but the classic way to deal with them (as taught by grandmas and other founts of psychological wisdom) is to tell yourself before you get to sleep that if you have the dream you will turn round and look at what is chasing you. Usually what happens is that we can't do it the first time the dream reoccurs, and maybe not even the second, but if we keep on programming our psyches that this is what we are going to do then it works. We suddenly remember in the dream that we want to turn round and see our pursuer and we do it. Usually, what we find behind us is not a huge terrifying monster but a much smaller entity that shrinks in size and looks quite normal once we have confronted it. This is usually the end of such dreams and the beginning of new self-knowledge coming into consciousness. We discover that some aspect of ourselves that we were afraid of is not so bad after all – and if we face it, it shrinks in importance.

EXPOSURE

Another common dream theme is finding ourselves in a social situation and discovering we are naked. Knowing as much as you do about the shadow, you can guess that this reflects a fear of exposure. We are terrified of being found out, of being exposed, of people seeing our failings. A similar dream is that we are giving a large public lecture – and we suddenly realize we have forgotten our notes and have nothing to say. The unconscious fear is the same – that beneath the veneer of competence and acceptable persona, we are shallow and have much to hide. What confronting the threatening monster in our dreams teaches us is that our dark side is not as bad as we think it is. This is why we suggest that you perform some of the exercises in this book while standing in front of a mirror. Inside our heads, all manner of small problems and minor negative attributes assume enormous significance. We expend huge effort in hiding aspects of ourselves that others would barely notice. Confronting ourselves in a mirror helps to bring our internal worries into external reality, where we can be more realistic about them.

To help you think about what you are afraid of exposing, try the exercise below.

1   What am I most afraid of finding out about myself?

2   What am I most afraid of other people finding out about me – my partner, my mother, my father, my children, my best friend, my boss?

3   What is the biggest lie I have ever told – to my partner, my mother, my father, my children, my best friend, my boss?

4   Now look at what you are hiding – from yourself and others. Is it the same thing, or different things?

5   Why are you hiding what you are hiding?

6   Now ask yourself: do you really need to hide it? And is there a way you can avoid hiding things from people in the future.

7   Ask yourself: what would I need to change about myself so that there was nothing to hide? Would I need to be less ambitious, more honest, more open, more willing to change my image?

8   Now ask yourself a final question: which is worse – what you are hiding or the qualities that you could express but which are suppressed because of what you are hiding?

9   The last question is a complicated and subtle one. The answer might not come straight away. If it does not, try writing it on a small piece of paper and putting it under your pillow. See if you wake up in the morning with the answer. When we are asleep, the unconscious works on unsolved problems – hence the

'Eureka' effect when we suddenly realize the solution to a problem just as soon as we stop worrying about it. Notice what you dream. The answer may be right there.

⩓⩔

NEW PARTS OF THE PSYCHE

A common dream is one in which we find ourselves in a house. The house is partly familiar but suddenly we find there is a whole series of additional rooms that we did not know about. Sometimes rooms will be furnished, sometimes not. Sometimes other people are there, but more often not. If you are thinking of moving house, the house dream may connect with your real life situation, but if you are not, the house may well symbolize your own psyche. Your dream is telling you that you have unexplored qualities that you are not utilizing. Maybe it is time to open the door to them. The furnishings or lack of them may give you clues. Does the room contain beautiful furniture and pictures – or a library? Is there a lot of empty space? Is this what you need in your life – space? Are there people there? Do you need to grow closer to others?

Another image of our psyche that can appear in dreams is that of a cave. We associate caves with the deep and hidden. They are mysterious places that lead to the underworld. They go deep down into the heart of our mother the Earth and are places of initiation. This exercise is based on the work of Italian psychotherapist Roberto Assagioli. The cave imagery is drawn from an exercise we first heard used by therapist Ellie Baker.

⋙ Something to try ⋘
INTO THE CAVE

For this exercise, you will need to be able to lie down somewhere warm and comfortable with dim lighting. You will need some large sheets of drawing paper and some colored pencils or pens. You should allow about an hour and a half for the exercise. You could read the exercise and visualize each instruction in turn, in which case you may like to write or type the exercise onto a sheet of paper in large print that you can read in dim lighting. Alternatively, you could read the instructions onto a tape, leaving gaps for the visualization. If you are taping the exercise, leave at least two to three minutes between each instruction.

1 Relax and go within yourself. Let your breathing settle down and let all the busy thoughts of the world drift away. Let yourself sink gently into stillness.

2 When you are ready, you find yourself on a warm summer's evening in a beautiful place in nature. The sun is sinking and the birds are beginning their evening song. All is warm and at peace. You are at home in this place.

3 You notice that a figure is coming towards you. This is a guide who will take you to meet safely with aspects of yourself that you have buried or neglected.

4 The guide approaches you. The guide may be male, female, animal, a being of light, or in some other form. You greet your guide who tells you that you will be guided to a nearby cave. You go with your guide to find the cave.

5 At the entrance to the cave, your guide indicates that you are to enter alone while he or she waits for you and keeps watch at the entrance.

6 You hear sounds within the cave that indicate presences inside and you go in.

7 Inside the cave, you encounter a person, animal or being that represents a hidden, lost or forgotten aspect of yourself. Sit quietly with this lost aspect of yourself and ask it what you need to know. What does this aspect of yourself need from you?

8 When this conversation comes to a close, you may find that another hidden aspect of yourself approaches you. Take time now to talk to this second being in the same way as the first.

9 When you have finished your conversation, you may sense that you can go deeper into the cave to access further parts of your being. If this seems appropriate, do so. If you have learned enough at this time, then begin to get ready to depart.

10 You return to the cave entrance where your guide is waiting to lead you home. You may find that your hidden self or selves have accompanied you to the entrance. Fill your heart with respect and love for them, and thank them for showing themselves to you at this time and bid them farewell, knowing that now you have encountered them, you can go back to the cave to talk with them whenever you wish.

11 Allow your guide to lead you back to the place in nature where you started the exercise. Thank your guide for assisting you on

your journey and in your own time return to your room in the everyday world.

12 Make the light brighter and record your experiences by drawing them. You might also want to write down some key words to help remind you of your experience.

More about Sarah: Sarah's cave journey

This is what happened when Sarah, a Buddhist nun, did the cave exercise. She found herself standing by the water's edge of a muddy inlet. Around her was tropical forest. The air was hot, humid, and filled with the sound of birds. A canoe glided across the still water towards her and she saw that the person paddling the canoe was a South American shaman. He landed and took her along the shore to a cave near the water's edge. Inside the cave, she found a large dark brown mother bear. The she-bear's eyes gleamed yellow in the darkness. The bear was leaning back against the cave wall allowing her cubs to play all over her. Sarah found that her consciousness was switching between her normal human form and that of the she-bear. Sometimes she was the she-bear and sometimes she was Sarah. The bear had no fear of her, nor she of it. Sarah felt the cubs feeding from her breasts. The sensation was extraordinary – fur, claws and tiny teeth – not the normal thing she would welcome, but she found it a marvelous sensation. As she sat leaning on the cave wall, the cubs feeding from her, another figure appeared from the darkness at the back of the cave – a dark skinned Tantric dancer who performed the most beautiful and sensual dance.

For Sarah the neglected aspects of herself were sensual, sexual and maternal, but also intensely physically strong and fierce. Sarah remembered in that moment that while she always thought of herself as timid, other people in her community had told Sarah that they found her intimidating. Sarah realized that in fact she was just like the bear – both fierce and shy. Sarah realized that she needed to access these neglected aspects of her being and that she must stop living so much in her head and more in the whole of her body. She needed to reclaim part of herself – her sensual, feeling self.

Accessing material from our dreams helps us communicate with the unconscious. It is also accessed through creative exploration.

More about Chris' dark side

As part of my training in transpersonal therapy, we were asked to draw our shadows. My first reaction was that this was stupid. I felt exposed and unwilling to show my shadow to others. A guided visualization took us into a house to open a door to an unknown room. Inside we would find our shadows. I opened the door and there was a man in black sitting at a rickety table, reading by candlelight. He was my age, but bearded, wearing late medieval costume with a strange old-fashioned foursquare cap on his head. He was poring over a rare book and was surrounded by bookshelves. Large books were stacked haphazardly on the shelves, floor, table, everywhere. A whole wealth of knowledge was there. And I was shocked to realize that the man looked remarkably like my argumentative and highly academic brother.

Many people would be pleased to find a medieval scholar in their dark side. I wasn't. Often in families, siblings take on different roles. One is the brainy one; one is the people person. One is science, the other is arts. Partly this is due to natural talents, partly we choose to differentiate ourselves from our brothers and sisters to gain a clear identity. In my family, I was the people person, and now hidden inside me I found the dry, dusty reclusive academic. Surely this person couldn't be me?

It was a long time before I could pay attention to the sage and his books. I was in the middle of therapy training and later trained in shiatsu. I was having to pay a lot of attention to my interpersonal skills and to learning Chinese medicine. The love of other books had to be hidden away. It was only when I began postgraduate work in Renaissance Studies that I remembered this picture and found it again. I could now pay attention to the needs of this thinking self.

⪌⪋ Something to try ⪌⪋

DRAWING YOUR DARK SIDE

Drawing, painting and writing are all ways we can use to explore our dark side. Try drawing or painting an image of your dark side. What does it look like? What are its surroundings like? What clothes does it wear? The image will give you clues about aspects of yourself that you are not utilizing and all these aspects can be transformed into positive ones. By drawing, we begin to make links to these hidden aspects of ourselves. When we link with them, we can listen to their needs.

⪌⪋

BRIGHT SIDE

One way that some shadow books deal with the dark side is to tell you that yes, you have a dark side, but that you are also a wonderful person full of infinite potential. This is true, but a danger is that facing the dark side can become an ego trip in itself. 'Shadow work' as spoken by some people can have an irritatingly pretentious ring. 'What wonderful people we are, because we alone have faced the shadow,' is the unspoken message. 'Look I was such a mess and now I'm redeemed and wonderful and can help you – for a fee.'

We would say something more prosaic, boring and true: dealing with shadow is an ongoing process. Our psyche constantly deceives us about our intentions. The trick is to learn to spot the self-deceptions – and then maybe we can stop playing such complex games. It is not easy to face up to the shadow, but it is also honest, real and empowering. We are empowered by discovering that we are not perfect. It makes us more able to tolerate the imperfections of others. We become more able to shrug our shoulders and to laugh a little at the convoluted thinking of humankind – even when it hurts us. And laughter – at oneself, the foibles of others and of the world – is one of the most healing things of all.

However, while not sending you off on some ego trip, it is important to recognize the qualities latent within us. Projection is not just of the negative qualities we do not want to own. We project onto other people the qualities we would like to have ourselves. We can delude ourselves into thinking we are much better people than we are, but we can be equally deluded that we are much worse. If we admire brave people, it is because we would like to be brave. Wanting to be brave is not the same thing as being brave, but it is a start. We cannot be something unless we want to be it. Letting into our conscious psyche the good qualities that we have run away from or have been too afraid to manifest is like opening the shutters of an old mansion that has not been lived in for many years. At first, we are afraid of what we might find, but as sunlight streams into the empty dusty rooms, we find they are not so scary after all. We can venture a little further – we can open the windows and let in some air. We can start to fantasize a little – supposing these rooms were mine, even just one of them. How would I furnish it? What would I do here? We start to grow a little and to accept that maybe we are a little more than we thought. We look into the mirror bravely – and maybe we like some of what we see.

⋙ Something to try ⋙
LOOKING ON THE BRIGHT SIDE

Here is an exercise to help you think about an undiscovered country – the country of your mind and soul.

1 Here is a list of words. They describe positive qualities. Try going through the list word by word, saying, 'I am (the word).'

adventurous	determined	just
assertive	diplomatic	kind
authentic	discreet	mature
balanced	energetic	open
brave	entertaining	organized
caring	flexible	relaxed
clever	forgiving	responsible
committed	generous	self-reliant
competent	happy	sexy
considerate	hard-working	warm
cooperative	honest	
creative	innovative	

2 How does it sound to describe yourself in this way – exactly right, totally off target, or something you could grow into? Is there a time when you manifested the quality? Would you like

to do so again? If you were to manifest this quality, where and when would you do so?

3 Obviously, you cannot be everything at once. Find the five qualities that most appeal to you that you would like to manifest more. Think about where you can manifest them in your life and how you would like to do it. Then begin. What you are doing psychologically is expanding your boundaries. You are giving yourself scope to grow.

By completing this exercise, you have started to confront a lost side of yourself – a side that has more potential than you think. You have started to see your golden shadow – a lopsided, slightly tarnished halo on a somewhat dirty angel. Shadow is about aspects of ourselves that we are unwilling to own. Some of these will be negative qualities, but some will be positive. It's just that our particular life circumstances suppressed this positive quality. Some of the best bits of ourselves are undiscovered country – beautiful country – that we have not yet dared to explore.

☆

FIVE THINGS TO REMEMBER

1 The shadow sets many small traps for us. Don't fall into the trap of becoming egotistical about dealing with your shadow.

2 Dealing with shadow is an ongoing process, but once we have insights about our shadows then we can start to change.

3 We exaggerate our negative qualities and fail to notice some of the most positive aspects of our personalities. Remember you have a lopsided halo as well as a shadow.

4 Your unconscious mind will try to help you on your journey of growth. Remember to remember your dreams.

5 Hidden in the unconscious is our potential, the life unlived. You are full of unrealized potential.

12) Transformation

*It is only when we have the courage to face things
exactly as they are, without any self-deception or illusion,
that a light will develop out of events, by which the
path to success must be recognized.*

Richard Wilhelm, trans. *I Ching: Book of Changes*

In the first chapter of this book, we talked about change. Why is it worth trying to know and come to terms with our negativity? Those who come to terms with their negativity, who learn to recognize it and to diminish its power in their lives, are doing something beneficial for themselves, but also for the collective psyche – society as a whole. In Chinese Taoist philosophy, the Yin Yang symbol shows us the constant change that is ever present in our universe. Nothing is static.

We talk about something, or someone, being as solid as a rock, but even rock is a swarming mass of molecules that are in a constant process of being built up and broken down. Changing shadow stuff isn't easy – if you try to do too much at once. Changing bit by bit is much easier. Remember the Zen master and the doorknob in chapter 1? Society is made up of individuals. If we as individuals can remove just one speck of tarnish from the doorknob, the light will shine a little more brightly than before.

This book is to help you understand what the shadow and dark side are and to help you recognize your own shadow and dark side. Once you know yourself better, it is possible to begin to change. We can be aware of the 'voice in the head' that puts us down and we can tell it to get lost. We can be aware of our anger and frustration and think about the real causes rather than taking them out on our partners. And if our partners are the cause, we can learn to take a deep breath and say, 'It makes me feel really angry when you do that. I think we need to talk about it.' You can learn to give yourself permission to say, 'Just a moment – this isn't right. I think you are taking advantage of me here.' Instead of fuming about being mistreated but not wanting to cause a problem by saying so, you can learn that it's ok to assert yourself and that it's not good for other people to be selfish and uncaring. You can learn to recognize the dark side in others and know when to say, 'Stop!' You in turn can recognize the negative side of your personality and say, 'Ok, that's me, but I don't have to act it out.' 'I don't have to be a dependent wimp: now I am a grown up.' 'I am physically strong and can use my anger and strength to frighten my partner, but I know I won't feel good about myself afterwards. Maybe I owe it to myself to do things differently. Maybe this behavior doesn't really get me where I want to be.' You do not have to let life sweep over you. Instead, you can say yes to life and allow the forward momentum of the life force, which is ever seeking evolution and growth, to take you where you want to go.

Taoist Yin Yang symbol

The Chinese Taoist Yin Yang symbol is a good one for our individual psyches. The bright white part is the ego, what we know and accept about ourselves. The dark spot in the white is what we know and dislike about ourselves. The dark spot should be small, but if we are depressed or have fallen into patterns of negative thinking, the black spot will expand and swamp the white. The black half of the Yin Yang symbol is the unknown – all that we do not know about ourselves. Some of it is dark, but within the dark is a bright, shining spot like a moon in the darkest night. This is the hidden treasure within the psyche, the part we have locked away. We all love treasure stories and mystical quests because they are a symbol of life itself. Each one of us has our own hidden treasure. The fun, joy, terror and thrill of life are to go on our own personal quest to find it.

⊰⧉⊱

THE WARRIOR WITHIN

The true self seeks to make the dark side conscious, even while our egos try to hide it. Our true self wants us to be whole and since it has a wiser perspective than the ego, it realizes that within the dark side are seams of unmined gold. What are the positive qualities that we are likely to find in the shadow?

We often find our courage in the dark side. This is the part of us that refuses to be daunted. It is the bloody-minded part of us that refuses to give in, that will not accept injustice, that has a stubborn determination to achieve what we want to achieve. Women especially can be discouraged from expressing this fearless side of ourselves – which is why we love our gutsy heroines.

SCARLETT O'HARA

Gone with the Wind, with screenplay by Sidney Howard, based on Margaret Mitchell's famous novel, was one of the most popular films ever made. Released in 1939 as one of the first color movies, its starring character is the dark-haired, sexy, unscrupulous and strong-minded sixteen-year-old, half-Irish Southern belle, Scarlett O'Hara. She inspires us much more than her cousin, the goody-goody and mousy Melanie. Only Scarlett can capture the heart of the film's hero Captain Rhett Butler. Scarlett is bad. She survives the Civil War, in which she has to shoot a drunken soldier who tries to rape cousin Melanie, and then seduces her younger sister's beau in order to save the family plantation Tara, named after the seat of the High Kings of Ireland, from carpetbaggers. She loses her third husband Rhett Butler, only to realize that she loved him all along – or is it, we suspect, that Scarlett only values what she has to fight for? In the film's final scene as Rhett abandons her, Scarlett turns her thoughts to Tara, the land and home that have never failed her.

'Tara! Home! I'll go home, and I'll think of some way to get him back! After all – tomorrow is another day!'

With this famous last line, the camera closes up to Scarlett's tear-stained face and then into an earlier shot, a last long view of Scarlett standing alone under a gnarled tree with Tara in the background, a heroine who will never admit defeat. Yes, Scarlett will live to fight again and our pulses race with her.

Our gutsy side is not ladylike or feminine and we can try to reject it, but in the competitive world in which we live today, we need our inner determination if we are to get the jobs we want to support our families, and to get the partner that we want and deserve. Within the dark side is courage.

Men can be equally convinced that part of their psyche that is valuable should be suppressed. Men are still discouraged from showing that they care and from expressing their true feelings. Feeling requires courage. We only hide what we are afraid of and fear is disempowering. It can be scary to admit that you love someone, that they have the power to hurt you, that it really matters to you that they care about you, but it is honest and true, and honesty gives us courage.

⌇

WITHDRAWING THE PROJECTIONS

Acknowledging our dark side means that we must stop projecting it onto others. We have to own our negative qualities instead of convincing ourselves that it is always other people who are selfish, cruel, uncaring, aggressive, dominating and out for what they can get. Unacknowledged qualities and energies must go somewhere. When we refuse to see our worst faults in ourselves, then we see them in other people.

In one study, a group university of students was asked to complete rating scales for undesirable traits such as meanness, obstinacy and untidiness (very undesirable if you have to share a room with someone). They were asked to rate first themselves and then other students they knew. The researchers compared the ratings that people had given themselves with the ratings that others had given them. Some people rated themselves in much the same way as their friends rated them. They had accurate self-perceptions. Others rated themselves as generous, flexible and tidy – but their peers saw them as mean, obstinate and untidy. Those who rated themselves well, but who were rated badly by their peers, tended to rate other students badly. They saw them as having all the undesirable qualities they were refusing to acknowledge in themselves. In other words, they were projecting their negative qualities onto others.

In order to escape from the shadow, we must own it. We must withdraw the shadow aspects of ourselves that we have projected onto others – whether other individuals or other social groups – and we must own qualities that we dislike. This has a number of virtues, the first of which is honesty. Withdrawing projections allows us to see the world as it really is. We look into the mirror of truth.

⤜⤛

RECOGNIZE, ACCEPT AND BEFRIEND

The shadow appears frequently in fairy tales and their modern equivalent children's novels, and fantasy and sci-fi movies and TV series. Novels, TV and film have become disseminators of modern morality tales that convey society's norms and values. What would have once been conveyed through tribal initiation myths and later by religious teachings is now often told through the fiction of page and screen. At the end of workshops on the dark side, we often read part of Ursula le Guin's *Earthsea Trilogy*.

This is written as a children's story, but it describes a sophisticated psychological battle between ego and shadow. Ged is a young trainee wizard who succumbs to the ego temptation to show off; something we all do from time to time. Showing off usually has unpleasant results. We feel uncomfortable with ourselves afterwards and have a feeling of 'decenteredness', what Buddhists would call *dhukka*. Ged's discomfort is more extreme. He does something that goes against the natural order of things. He tries to bring a dead spirit back to life. Ged's downfall starts because his ego is angry after a put down from one of the young sorcerers. He challenges the young man, Jasper, to a duel of power. His friend Vetch tries to save him from his folly, 'Will you be a man and drop this now – come with me,' but Ged is too stupid to listen. Wise though he is in magic, he is not wise about himself. He has allowed himself to be drawn into a trap – a magical display from which his ego will not let him back down. The results are disastrous. Ged succeeds in raising the dead spirit but he releases something else at the same time – a black and nameless thing that can only be sent back by the powerful head of the academy of wizards, and the effort costs the great master his life.

Jasper's role is not as negative as it seems. He is acting here as the trickster shadow. In the human world, the shadow often precipitates a crisis that leads to growth. The will to grow and evolve is so strong that it defies the ego's attempts to stop it. Something must give. Jasper lures Ged into revealing a side of himself that is there, but as yet Ged is unconscious of it. Ged is horribly scarred by the encounter and takes months to recover. When he is sufficiently recovered to take his oath of allegiance to the new chief wizard, his new lord speaks to him of the shadow he has raised.

'The power you had to call it gives it power over you: you are connected. It is the shadow of your arrogance, the shadow of your ignorance, the shadow you cast. Has a shadow a name?'

Eventually, with the help of his friend Vetch, Ged sails out to a grey mist-laden sea and the shadow comes to him. As it advances towards him, it takes on many faces – his father's, his enemy Jasper's, whose taunts led him to unleash the shadow, and then finally as it is – a black and sickening thing. And in the silence as the two stand face-to-face, Ged names the shadow – and its name is Ged. As he recognizes this dark and frightful thing as part of himself he accepts it. The two aspects of himself merge. Ged takes hold of his shadow, the black self that reaches out to him. Light and darkness meet, and join, and become one. Ged has acknowledged his inner darkness and become whole. Ged and his friend Vetch sail home and their hearts are joyful.

The boat that takes Ged and Vetch to the edge of darkness and back again is called Lookfar. The challenge of the shadow is for us to look far – deep into the deepest wells of our being, high into the dark and starry night, wide across the world, and at the dawn of the rising sun. And if we look far we may see that all creatures are our brothers and sisters and that together we share a great adventure, the journey of transformation, of hope and dawn, of sorrow and sunset, all the way to the sunless sea and safely home again.

DEVELOPING WHOLENESS

... this thing of darkness! Acknowledge mine.

The magician Prospero in *The Tempest*, Act V, Scene 1

In William Shakespeare's play *The Tempest*, the magician Prospero is banished to a remote island where he lives with his daughter Miranda and two spirits. Ostensibly, Ariel is the airy, intellectual, good spirit. Caliban is the shadow. He is a cannibal and represents Prospero's negative and primitive dark side. Caliban continually rebels from the control of Prospero, who represents the conscious ego. It is not until the play's final resolution that Prospero admits that Caliban is his 'thing of darkness'. Once this has occurred Prospero and Miranda, his feminine side, can be saved from their isolation and life move forward.

Realization of the shadow is a step on the way to what Carl Jung called individuation, the integration of the personality. We become whole by acknowledging all the hidden aspects of ourselves – good and bad – and by finding a new center of consciousness that psychologists call the self, or sometimes the true self. To free ourselves from the grip of the shadow, we need to hear a voice within us that is not based on fear, anger, competitiveness, jealousy, or any of the other negative emotions that drive human beings. Spiritual practices such as meditation, prayer, or silent retreat are designed to help us hear this clear and true voice. To finally confront the shadow we need a new perspective in which shadow can play an integrated role. This is not the perspective of the ego – that person whom we thought we were. Shadow is the opposite of ego and for the two to live comfortably together, there must be a third and reconciling viewpoint that helps them appreciate each other's positive qualities.

That third perspective is that of the true self. To find this perspective, you need to be able to learn to listen to its voice.

LISTENING TO THE VOICE OF THE TRUE SELF

For this exercise, you need quiet and privacy. Allow about an hour. You will need four pieces of large plain paper and four different-colored pens.

1. Write a heading on each of the four pieces of paper, using the colored pens. The headings are: Mind, Body, Emotions and Observer. Sit on the floor and put the Observer paper in front of you, Mind to your right, Emotions to the left and Body behind you to form a cross. Place the pens on top of their respective pieces of paper.

2. The Observer is wise, compassionate and non-judgmental. The Observer helps us get an overview of our life. To become the Observer, we must make a link with our true Self. Focus for a few minutes on the wise being that lies hidden deep within your psyche. You may find it helpful to imagine being bathed in light.

3. Turn around to face the paper headed 'Body'. It is important for you to move. This works far better than moving the pieces of paper. Ask yourself the following questions:
   • What are the strengths of my body?
   • What are its weaknesses?
   • What needs does it have that have not been met?
   • What step can it take to meet that need?

4 Spend ten minutes thinking about these questions and write notes on your paper about what comes to you.

5 Turn to face your Observer paper again. Clear your psyche of the insights from your body and get in touch with your wise compassionate self.

6 Now turn to your left to the paper headed 'Emotions'. Ask yourself:
   • What are my emotional strengths?
   • What are my emotional weaknesses?
   • What emotional needs do I have that have not been met?
   • What steps can my emotions take to meet those needs?

7 Write your notes. After ten minutes or so, turn to the Observer position again and reconnect to your wise self.

8 Now do the same for 'Mind'. Turn to the Mind paper and ask yourself:
   • What are the strengths of my mind?
   • What are its weaknesses?
   • What intellectual needs do I have that have not been met?
   • What steps can my mind take to take to meet those needs?

9 Make your notes and then return at the end to your Observer position.

10 Next, turn to Body, Mind and Emotions in turn, in whatever order you wish. Ask each in turn: 'Are you satisfied with our way of life? If not, is there any one thing you would like to change so that we can co-operate creatively and incorporate this into our lifestyle?'

11 Finally, turn to face the Observer place. You may have been asked to make some changes. You, the wise Observer at the center, should consider these requests carefully and realistically. Can you make them and, if not, why not? If you can make the changes, when will you make them?

12 When you have reached your decisions, stay facing the Observer place and thank Body, Emotions and Mind for their assistance and insights. If you cannot make the changes they request, explain why. If you can, make it a promise.

13 During the course of the next month, use the insights you have gained from this exercise to make positive changes in your life. You are not your body, emotions or mind. They are part of you, but are not the whole. Within you, there is a deeper, wiser person that is your true self. The self is a source of loving wisdom and wise insight. Take a few moments each day to be still and to listen to the wise voice within.

Individuation is sometimes written about as though it is a one-off event. Suddenly the magical moment comes and we are wholly integrated beings. If we were to die at that point, then this would be true, but life of course is an ongoing process. We are constantly faced with fresh and unexpected challenges that require us to use new or existing qualities. However, if we have begun the journey to self-knowledge we will have more to draw on and the challenges of life, while not easy, will be easier.

⌇⌇ SPIRITUALITY AND SHADOW

This is not a religious book. We are not advocating a particular spiritual tradition, or indeed any spiritual tradition at all. Religious traditions have all attempted to tackle the issue of the shadow. Some mechanisms devised by religious traditions have been helpful. Traditions as diverse as indigenous religions, the Quakers, and the Catholic Church have devised ways for people to admit wrongdoing and guilt, all of which can help us face the shadow. In Catholicism, in the anonymity of the confessional, people are encouraged to face the dark side of their psyches, to own it and so liberate energy for change. Indigenous traditions and the Quakers have public ceremonies of admission of wrongdoing whereby individuals are encouraged to be open about themselves amongst a supportive community. Group therapy, Alcoholics Anonymous, and other psychological support groups have all adopted these techniques and found them useful.

Buddhism approaches the dark side of the psyche in a slightly different way from other spiritual traditions. In theistic traditions that worship a personal deity or deities, people might be encouraged to face their dark side because this is pleasing to the Divine. This may be true, but it is not necessarily helpful to people living in secular societies who do not believe in gods. Buddhism is a philosophy of life rather than a religion that venerates a deity. It teaches a pragmatic approach that will be more in accord with the life experience of many in Western society today. From a Buddhist perspective, it is good to do something about the dark side because it is dysfunctional. If we do not, then our thoughts, feelings and perceptions are distorted. We get things wrong, we misinterpret things, and we cause ourselves suffering – *dhukka*. Dark side behavior is irrational and unskillful behavior. Learning to behave in more skilful ways is a bit like ironing out the problems in a golf stroke, relearning to swim using a more effective breathing technique, or coping with an up-graded computer. There is an initial learning phase in which we are uncertain about how to do formerly familiar tasks and then we find that we can do them much better than before.

We can see when we are projecting our emotions and thoughts onto others and when we are not. Buddhism talks about how *papanca*, the proliferation of associations, ideas, attitudes and emo-tions, distorts our perception so we no long see clearly. To give an example, we see someone, this creates a visual image of him or her, and we start to speculate about this person. What kind of person is this? What is the person's likely attitude towards us? Is this a friend or an enemy? Aspects of the person's dress, mannerisms, ethnicity and social class will all trigger certain associations for us. These may not be conscious but they will affect how we behave. We may con-clude that this person thinks himself superior to us, so we do not go up and speak to him. Later he goes home and talks about that un-friendly person today who did not speak to him once. The dark side works in this way. We project erroneous images onto one another and communication is distorted. When we start to own our shad-ows we start to recognize what belongs to another person and what we are projecting onto that person.

Wholeness comes from seeing all of ourselves – darkness and light. Some people are egotists inclined to see only the light. In the night, their eyes are blind. Others are depressives inclined to see only the shadows. Like vampires, they cannot bear the brightness of the noonday sun. We can be truly at peace with ourselves when we recognize our weaknesses and strengths, pluses and minuses, shadow and light.

Many books on the shadow discuss the dark side of the personality in moral terms, as good and evil. We prefer to discuss the dark side of the personality in much simpler and pragmatic terms. This does not mean that there is no moral or religious aspect to shadow, after all, the world's great religious have agonized over evil for years. Whether that agonizing has made the world a better place, however, is open to doubt. We say that it is good to face the shadow because shadow behavior is dysfunctional. It gets in the way and stops us living our lives as well as we could. It stops us being real and authentic people – which should be the goal of all spiritual systems – and makes us false, weak and dysfunctional people. Shadow stops us using our talents and creates barriers between other people and us. To get rid of the barriers we need to take down the fences and be more open about ourselves. This openness needs to start with ourselves. We need to look into the mirror and see what is there.

Acknowledging the dark side: more of Sarah's story

Spiritual traditions that teach us to examine our thought processes and how we behave can help us acknowledge our dark sides, but this does not mean that spiritual traditions will produce perfect people. Remember Sarah?

After fifteen years as a nun, Sarah was a well-known teacher in her Buddhist tradition. She traveled widely in North America and Europe leading retreats, giving lectures and representing her tradition at interfaith events. Her order was going through enormous transitions as it adapted itself to the West and to an equal role for women. Sarah was a role model for many young women and men joining the order and she had become the leading person of her generation. She was one of the most senior Western initiates and was rapidly reaching a position that no women had reached before. Sarah's future seemed mapped out for her by her teachers and at age 36 she saw herself as totally dedicated to the way of life she had embraced 15 years before.

Life changed for Sarah when she attended an interfaith conference. One of the Catholic representatives was a former monk and she felt strongly attracted to him. They began talking during the first morning break and she felt she had known him for years. Since he knew nothing about her, she found herself for the first time in many years explaining herself and her life. As she told him something about herself, she had a strange sensation. It was as though she was describing someone else's life and not her own. She found this highly disturbing and while she allowed her friendship with the former monk to develop, she began to concentrate on asking him about his life rather than discussing hers. They talked in-depth about why he had left his order, about issues of celibacy and about his desire to have children. At this point, Sarah experienced another moment of extreme disorientation. She felt dizzy and the walls of the room began to close in on her and then expand into the distance. She said nothing about this but was concerned enough to think that she must do something about it.

Sarah's position as a teacher had left her feeling inwardly isolated. She was the most senior person in her own community and there was no one she could easily confide in. She was treated as a guru. Her function was to listen to other people's problems and her own teachers were based in another country. As a way of finding out more about herself, Sarah enrolled in a series of transpersonal psychology workshops held in a city where few people knew her. She attended the workshops under her birth name (Sarah) rather than her Buddhist name, wore ordinary clothes, hoped that her very short hair did not make her look odd, and told no one about her role as a spiritual teacher.

Through the workshops, Sarah began looking at her shadow and came to be deeply sorry for the way she had treated her former boyfriend before she became a nun. She still had his parents' address and wrote him a letter apologizing for her behavior. The letter was more of a therapeutic exercise for Sarah than an attempt to recontact her boyfriend and having sent the letter, Sarah immediately regretted what she had done. She could see that in trying to open herself to shadow, she was practicing another complex loop of self-deception. She was using her boyfriend again – this time to make her feel better about herself.

To her surprise, Sarah's former boyfriend got her letter and replied. Since they had last met, he had been married and divorced, and had done a lot of work on himself. His letter was tender, loving, forgiving and humorous. He shared some of his own past shadow actions with her and helped her see that maybe her shadow was not as bad as she had thought. She realized that her ex-boyfriend, whom she had always secretly looked down on as a materialist, had a great deal of human wisdom and she experienced a new liberation within herself – she began to see herself as really part of suffering humanity, rather than set apart as a spiritual teacher of others.

We do not yet know the end of Sarah's story. She has maintained her friendship with the former Catholic monk and her former boyfriend has come to visit her at the Buddhist community. She knows that she has a very strong urge to have a child, and knows that she will have to make a decision fairly soon about that. She is not clear whether she wants to sacrifice the opportunity of being a mother or the work that she has put into the order. She is beginning to have a vision of another type of Buddhist community for people with children. She is not sure if either possible relationship that is open to her would fit in with that plan, although both men are showing an interest in Buddhism. Sarah has discovered a lot more about herself over the past two years. Discovering parts of herself she had repressed has given her some complex choices rather than making her life simpler, but she has no regrets. For the first time in years, she feels completely alive.

≳⁄≲

DARK SIDE STATEMENTS

At the end of workshops or one-to-one sessions on the dark side, we ask people to write their own personal Dark Side Statement and share it. In group work, speaking aloud about our Dark Side Statement gives it concrete reality, but in the anonymity of a group of non-threatening strangers. This allows us to experiment with openness and start to practice how we want to live our lives in the future. By now, you will have some insights into the nature of your own dark side, so we suggest that you write your own Dark Side Statement, but before doing so, here are some statements to help you.

Some dark side statements
Alan the independent operator
My childhood was so over-controlled I never wanted anyone to be in control of my life ever again. But this has stopped me using my talents because I wouldn't take responsibility in organizations. I can fulfill my potential without compromising my need for freedom. In

future I will run my own business. The solution's so obvious, I don't know why I didn't think of it before.

Anne, whose sex life with her husband was unsatisfactory

My mother never spoke much about sex but I got the idea that she didn't enjoy it much. Somehow, I got the idea that women should be passive sexual partners and wait for men to do things to them. I'm going to take more responsibility for making our sexual relationship work. And I need to think about other areas of my life. I've always waited for things to happen to me, instead of making them happen. I don't think I'm achieving enough in my career and I need to do something about this. When I drew my dark side, I drew a medieval princess looking out of a tower. I don't know what this means yet, but I'm going to find out.

Chris

In childhood I found my father's and brother's intellectual arguments deeply upsetting and have avoided intellectual arguments ever since. This meant I refused to defend my ideas and I missed out on valuable opportunities. By acknowledging that I have an intellectual side and that I believe my ideas are right, I can have the courage of my convictions and can fulfil my creative potential.

John, who gave up playing the violin

I lack self-confidence and am easily influenced by other people's ideas about how I should live my life. My dark side tells me that those I love know best for me and if I don't behave in the way that they like, maybe they won't love me any more. I have to have the courage of my convictions and do what I want even if I fail. People who really love me will still love me if I fail. I am an adult now and not a child.

Kelly, the television presenter whose father left home when she was seven years old

When my father left I was devastated. Something inside me died but I couldn't let it show because my mother insisted we pretended that everything was all right. I couldn't let her down by saying how much I missed him. Since then I've never trusted men and have treated them badly. When I was a kid I wasn't in control of what happened to me, but now I'm a grown up. Starting today, I'm taking control of the rest of my life. I feel like my dark side is a kind of friend – although that sounds strange. It's like the story Vivianne read out about Ged. I feel as though I'm starting out on an exciting voyage and sailing a boat, the boat of my life, out into a wide open sea, and the different parts of me – dark side, bright side, the face I put on for the public – they're the crew and I'm the captain. Consciously I don't know where I'm going, but unconsciously I do.

Linda, who walked out on her boyfriend leaving a note and no forwarding address

It was a shitty thing to do, but it was the best I could manage at the time. And my dark side tells me it serves him right, even though I know that's not really true. I can forgive myself for not being perfect, but now I'm older and know more about myself, I'll treat people better.

Mario, who avoided exams and work evaluations

My dark side is cowardly and runs away from difficult situations and my macho Italian upbringing makes this difficult to admit – even to myself. Opting out when the going gets tough is hampering my career and relationships. Now I've admitted it, I can do something about it. And I'm excited by the idea. I know I need a challenge.

Peter, whose father wouldn't give him financial support for university

I know my father loves me but his ideas of what are right for me aren't always mine. It's easier for me to accept him as he is than it is for him to change. He came from a very poor background and struggled just to survive. He can't always understand where I'm going and what I want to do. My dark side says, poor me: other people have got supportive parents who help them. My bright side says I love my father, but he's not a perfect person. I'm going to have to make it on my own more than I need to, but I will succeed and when I have children I'll make sure I help them.

Philip, the son of a millionaire who, when he died, left all his money to his new wife

I spent all my life being dominated by my father because it was easier than making my own way. I have to face the fact that this was a mistake. I'm middle-aged and having to start again. My dark side tells me that if only I'd done things differently, my life would have been ok. My bright side tells me that I've an enormous amount of knowledge about the engineering business and I know how to run a business, so I'm going to get a bank loan and set up on my own. I've made a drawing of my bright side that shows someone breaking out of jail. For the first time in my life, I'm free.

Rod, the workplace bully

My father was a bully and as a boy I was taught that this was how to get your own way. I used to enjoy humiliating people but I don't like bullies and I'm going to stop my dark side turning me into one. I'm going to learn new ways of dealing with people, so I can like myself better.

Sarah, the Buddhist

My dark side deceives me and convinces me that I am a spiritual being above worldly considerations, when in fact I can be a vindictive bitch. But if I am open about my failings and my attempts to overcome them, in my role as a teacher I can be a valuable role model for others.

Suzie, whose mother kept her at an emotional distance

Because I didn't like myself much, I ate to fill the emptiness I felt inside. My dark side told me what a horrible fat ugly failure I was and I liked myself even less. Because I couldn't accept myself, I couldn't accept others. I was always hypercritical of them. My relationships were a failure because I wasn't a nice person to know, not because I was fat. I'm going to befriend myself and enjoy my own company instead of being scared to be alone. I will care for myself better and in constructive ways that make me happy. I will become the kind of person that I want to be with, then others will want to be with me too.

Tom, who changed careers

My dark side makes me ill rather than admit things about myself. I had to admit that some conventional and high-status career routes are just 'not me'. I didn't want to admit my interest in the arts because my father thought all men in the art world were queers. In fact, I have got issues about my sexuality and I am attracted to men. I want to get my career on track before I start to deal with this, but I know that this is the next stage of my journey.

Vivianne

My dark side is competitive. I like to do things better than everyone else and to be always right. If I allow my dark side to get away with it, I can feel jealous and disempowered by other people's success. If, instead, I allow their achievements to inspire me, I can achieve more than I ever possibly dreamed.

Wendy, the graphic designer

I allowed a boss to undermine my self-confidence because I didn't believe in myself. My mother always undermined me and I've depended too much on others' evaluations. Now I need to start making my own.

⌁

FREEDOM

When the dark side dominates our lives, we are held, bound and constrained. We have to hide part of ourselves and keep it secret. Secrets hold energy and when we have to keep part of our lives secret, then this is a heavy burden. Openness means being more open with others and with oneself. The first stage of growth can be like a personal confession. We admit certain things to ourselves. We open the locked drawers, closets and shuttered rooms, and we let in the light. Light makes shadows flee and the fears of the night shrink. When there is light, we can see things in perspective. We open ourselves to the possibility of finding our own personal quest, of moving forward in our lives, and of the revelation of our true purpose.

Think for a moment about the positive and negatives below and their opposites.

Negative		Positive		Result
Conceal	→	Reveal	=	Revelation
Hide	→	Seek	=	Quest
Withdrawn	→	Outgoing	=	Movement
Secret	→	Open	=	Inspiration
Blockage	→	Release	=	Energy

The first column belongs to the world of shadow, a world of darkness and limitation. It is about the secret hiding places of the soul, where we can rest and recuperate. Sometimes we need periods of gestation when we can hide away, but in order to move forward in our lives we need to enter into the world. The second column is the opposite of the first. It is what happens when we move forward and outwards, when we go out to embrace our destiny. The third column contains the results of the transformations that can occur when we leave the shadows and are willing to risk a little more exposure than before. When we are no longer held back by the burden of secret shames, inferiority feelings, guilt, and repressed or frozen emotions, then we are free. We return a little to childhood innocence, not in the sense that we are no longer responsible for past actions, but in the sense that we can allow ourselves to begin again. We can allow ourselves to regain our childhood curiosity and openness to new experience. We can allow ourselves to become truly alive.

By accepting and seeking to transform our dark sides, we and others have found an extraordinary source of energy, creativity and inner power. The dark side traps part of our psyches in negative patterns that go round and round in our lives and in our heads. By confronting what these patterns are about, we can change them and release the energy that they contain to grow in ways that we would never have imagined. Darkness is the place where the seed is fertilized and begins the process of growing into a beautiful plant. Out of the dark side comes positive energy, energy that can transform your life.

⩗⩗ Something to try ⩗⩗
WRITING YOUR DARK SIDE STATEMENT

Now try creating your own Dark Side Statement. Take a sheet of paper and write what your dark side prompts you to do and how you want to change it. You may want to make more than one statement, but once you have written them, choose one to work on first. Remember – change is easy, providing you do it a bit at a time.

You Dark Side Statement is a self-promise. Hide it on your computer or write it out neatly and put it in a place where you can find it. Have a look at it once a day on weekdays only – weekends are for rest and play. Noon is a good time, when the sun is at its brightest and the bright side is there to give us optimism. Check that you are keeping your self-promise and if you are not don't be self-punitive. Just keep trying and eventually you'll get there. Think doorknob!

☆

TEN FINAL THINGS TO HELP YOU TRANSFORM NEGATIVE INTO POSITIVE ENERGY

1 Know that it is possible.

2 Start from the outside in: clear out unwanted possessions from your home environment; get a book on Feng Shui and rid your home environment of negative energy. You will start to feel in control.

3 Do the exercises in this book and practice them: they will help you know yourself and change yourself.

4 The ancient Greeks said that a healthy mind comes from a healthy body. This is simple but true. Change your diet to a healthy one and know that your body deserves your loving care. Think of your body as a beautiful pet that you have been given to own. Exercise it, take it out to play. You want it to feel and look its best. Go to a color class and find out what colors suit you. Give away or throw out clothes that you discover do nothing to enhance your appearance.

5 Have fun with the universe: perform random acts of kindness – try one a week to start.

6 Take up meditation – vipassana or mindfulness meditation in Eastern traditions will teach you to cleanse the windows of your vision so that you can evaluate yourself and your experience realistically and learn to undo negative thinking.

7 Therapeutic work can help you, whether one-to-one or in weekend groups. Attend some workshops in Jungian, transpersonal or similar psychologies to get to know yourself.

8 Once a week, do something that you have never done before. New experiences help us grow. Simply going to work by a different route will expose you to different visual images.

9 Creative work can help us access our shadows. We are all creative – remember how children love to paint and draw. Keep a diary, draw and paint your dark and bright sides, or write about your dark side and how you want to change.

10 Remember that life is beautiful and fun. It doesn't always go our way, but when thing aren't going right, look at the night sky and remember that you live in a beautiful cosmos and it is wonderful to be a small part of it. Look at the sky again and remember that we are all made up of light and darkness, joy and sorrow, good and bad, optimism and realism. This creates a beautiful pattern. When we are stuck in a black hole we forget to look at the stars, but the stars are there. Look out and remember. Of all the millions of stars out there, hardly any have life forms like us. Conscious beings are rare and special and you are a conscious being. Rejoice in being human. It's a great thing to be.

Afterword

The dark side
quiz

How well do you know your Dark Side? A light-hearted look at the shadows.

1 A friend wins a large sum of money in a lottery. Are you:
   a. pleased for him – he deserves it? You ring up immediately and congratulate him.
   b. pleased – and just a little bit jealous – but you ring up immediately and congratulate him?
   c. unable to put the thought out of your mind that if only you'd bought the ticket, it would have been you?
   d. jealous as hell, but grit your teeth, ring up and congratulate him?
   e. furious and hate his guts? You'll never speak to him again.
   f. planning to emotionally blackmail him into giving you a loan.

2 Your friend's partner, whom you've always found attractive, gets drunk at a party and makes a pass at you. Do you:
   a. tell your friend's partner not to be so silly? He or she will regret it in the morning.
   b. enjoy a lingering kiss until struck by conscience and think better of it?
   c. slap him or her round the face and burst into tears?
   d. go straight to tell your friend? He or she should know what a potential cheat this person is.
   e. have a quickie in the back bedroom and hope your friend never finds out?
   f. tell him/her to ring you next week if they're serious?

3 You are parking in the office car park and reverse into the boss's car. His car is dented but yours is fine. Do you:
   a. admit to your boss what you've done?
   b. drive immediately to another parking space before anyone sees you and spend the rest of the day being anxious?
   c. tell your boss you dented his car unavoidably because you were swerving to avoid a runaway dog?
   d. drive immediately to another parking space and tell your boss you saw a white car reverse into his?
   e. tell your boss that your arch rival at work did it?
   f. tell your boss that your arch rival at work did it, *and* create supporting evidence?

4 Your home is robbed and you have to make an insurance claim. Do you:

   a. claim only for what was stolen?

   b. claim for what was stolen plus an item of jewellery that you lost on holiday but wasn't covered by insurance?

   c. claim for what was stolen plus a 25 per cent mark up because insurance is such a rip off?

   d. claim for what was stolen plus a new camera, stereo, computer and various other items that you want to own?

   e. make a large claim although nothing was stolen because the thief was disturbed?

   f. make a large claim although nothing was stolen because there never was a robbery? It's an insurance scam.

5 You are driving along the highway and a car comes up fast behind you and hangs on your tail. Do you:

   a. slow down and pull aside to let it pass?

   b. hang in the middle of the lane so the car can't get by?

   c. accelerate – no one's going to overtake you?

   d. accelerate, then turn your lights on so the car behind thinks you've braked – and then zoom away?

   e. slow down and pull aside to let it pass, then put your headlights on full and follow it, hanging in just behind?

   f. accelerate and then slow down and pull aside for the car to pass just before the radar trap around the corner?

6 You find a wallet on the floor in the office cloakroom. You look inside to find the owner and discover there's a lot of money inside and it belongs to someone who's always been unpleasant to you. Do you:
   a. return the wallet and the money?
   b. take half the money and leave the wallet lying where you found it?
   c. take all the money and leave the wallet lying where you found it?
   d. take the money and the wallet – it's got your fingerprints on it?
   e. take the money, wipe the wallet clean, and plant it in your boss's waste paper bin? You've been angling for her job for months.
   f. take the money, wipe the wallet clean, plant it in your boss's wastepaper bin, and when the owner discovers that the wallet is missing say, 'That's funny, I thought I saw a wallet in a strange place earlier. Now where was it? I know – the boss's wastepaper bin'?

7 You discover your partner's been cheating on you. Do you:
   a. explain that you've found out and sit down to discuss your future?
   b. confront him or her and suggest you go to see a counselor?
   c. confront him or her and insist it stops immediately?
   d. walk out and never speak to him or her again?
   e. confront your partner, be forgiving and then auction his or her CD collection on the net?
   f. think, 'Great – now I can have an affair with that person in the office that I've been lusting after for ages,' then confront your partner about his or her cheating?

8 You are supervising a student on a three-month placement with your department at work. She has a great idea that will save the department money. You refine the idea a bit and tell your boss about it. Your boss assumes the idea is yours and says you will get a large bonus for it at the end of the financial year. The student is leaving in a few days and will never find out. Do you:

a. tell your boss that the idea is the student's and suggest the bonus goes to the student?

b. tell your boss that the student's idea partially inspired you and that part of the bonus should go to her?

c. say nothing, but write the student a glowing and exaggerated reference?

d. say nothing, buy the student a large leaving present in compensation, and blush when she gives a speech saying what a wonderful supervisor you've been?

e. say nothing and take the credit and the bonus?

f. say nothing, take the credit and the bonus, and write the student a damning reference to make sure that she can never come back to your firm and find out?

9 Your difficult and demanding elderly mother tells you that she is going to change her will. She was going to leave all her money jointly to you and your brother, but now she wants to leave it all to you because your brother doesn't visit as much as you do. Your brother has large family responsibilities and lives a long way away. Do you:

a. explain how much your brother loves her but it's difficult for him to make the journey as often as you?

b. say nothing – it's her business what she does with her money?

c. think, 'Great, I'm the one who does all the work, it's only fair'?

d. start telling her all the negative things your brother has said about her in the past?

e. ring a lawyer to arrange the redrafting?

f. think, 'Great! I've spent months persuading my brother that he's not needed and now my plan's paying off'?

10 You are a freelancer. A non-profit-making organization has contacted you to ask if you could do a week's work for them at a reduced rate to help them meet the deadline for an important fund-raising campaign. You agree because you have no other work that week, but late on Friday afternoon a regular client phones you with a week's work at your usual commercial rate. Do you:

a. decide you must honor your commitment to the non-profit-making organization and turn down your commercial client?

b. ring around your friends to see if you can find someone else to do the non-profit-making organization's work?

c. ring the non-profit-making organization and explain that you can't afford to turn down your regular client, but you'll do their work the following week – which means their campaign will be late?

d. ring the non-profit-making organization and explain that you'll still come if they'll pay your commercial rate?

e. ring the non-profit-making organization on Monday morning and say that you're ill?

f. never find yourself in this situation? You never do cut price work, however good the cause.

11 You've a friend who copies everything you wear. He or she asks you about your latest outfit and wants to know where to buy one. Do you:

    a. take the opportunity to confront the situation and ask your friend why he or she does it?

    b. tell your friend where to buy it but ask your friend not to wear it when you're likely to be seen together?

    c. say you can't remember?

    d. lie and say you bought it on holiday abroad?

    e. say that they don't do large sizes?

    f. think, 'This person is highly suggestible. How can I use him/her?'

12 You and a friend make a pledge to give up smoking together. You have severe nicotine cravings. Do you:

    a. stick it out? You don't want to let your friend down.

    b. have the odd cigarette but tell your friend what you're doing? You don't want to lie about it.

    c. have the odd cigarette – after all, your friend will never know?

    d. give up giving up but don't tell your friend? You don't want to discourage him or her.

    e. give up giving up and smoke in front of your friend, telling him or her how great it is?

    f. keep telling your friend how difficult it is and is it all worth it? When your friend gives up giving up, give up as well and blame your friend.

13 You are house sitting for some friends while they're on holiday and break an expensive ornament. Do you:
    a. admit it, find out if it's covered by their insurance and if not then offer to buy a replacement?
    b. try to get a replacement?
    c. try to repair it so they won't notice?
    d. admit it but don't offer to replace it? Things get broken all the time and you were doing them a favor anyway.
    e. throw it away and if they notice, say, 'What ornament?'
    f. blame the cat?

14 You have been dating someone for two years and have talked together about marriage. You meet someone new on a business trip and fall in love. How do you tell your previous partner?
    a. Meet up face to face and tell the truth.
    b. Say that you need some personal space and have decided to go solo for a bit.
    c. Send an e-mail saying it's over.
    d. Make your old partner's life such hell that he or she dumps you.
    e. Turn up at a party with your new love.
    f. Carry on with both until life becomes too complicated.

15 Your spouse of three years thinks he or she is great in bed, but you are sexually unfulfilled. Do you:
    a. prepare an exotic candlelit meal, tell your partner how much you love him or her, and discuss the problem openly?
    b. rent some erotic videos and suggest you try out what you see?
    c. wait until he or she is out and masturbate while imagining your favorite fantasy?

d. suggest you take up swinging?

e. take a lover?

f. tell your partner that he or she is useless in bed and that you're leaving? When your mutual friends ask you why, you tell them.

16 You live in an apartment and your noisy upstairs neighbors make your life hell. Do you:

a. go upstairs and explain that the noise insulation isn't very good and ask if they could be less noisy late at night?

b. write a letter of complaint to the building's management company?

c. retaliate by vacuuming beneath their bedroom and singing loudly at 5am?

d. find a new apartment?

e. seethe inwardly and develop migraines but do nothing?

f. consult a local voodoo practitioner about a specially nasty hex?

17 You invite some vegetarian friends to dinner. Just before they arrive you realize you've put chicken stock in the vegetable casserole. It's too late to start making another meal. Do you:

a. explain the problem when they arrive and take them out to a restaurant?

b. dial for a home delivery pizza?

c. pretend that you never intended giving them dinner – it's drinks only?

d. say nothing and let them eat the casserole, hoping that they won't notice?

e. say nothing and if they notice, say, 'Isn't chicken vegetarian?'

f. let them eat it and gloat? Vegetarians are very irritating.

18 You and a close friend both work in the same field. He tells you about an exciting job he's just seen advertised and is going to apply for. You realize that it's the perfect job for you and if you apply you're more likely to get it because you have more experience. Do you:

a. not apply – it's his opportunity?

b. apply and tell your friend that you really want to try for it too?

c. apply but not tell him?

d. think quickly on your feet and say, 'What a coincidence! I'm applying for that as well'?

e. say, 'Oh, yes, I've been approached by a headhunter about that one. I'm already on the shortlist'?

f. discourage him from applying on the basis that he's got sufficient experience but you've heard a rumor that the firm's about to go bust? Then apply yourself.

SCORING

Score a=1, b=2, c=3, d=4, e=5, f=6.

Over 90: You know your dark side very well – in fact you're living it out. It doesn't sound as though you like other people very much or have much empathy with them. Think about the kind of real friend you would like to have and what the differences are between the ways in which you behave and what you would want from a friend. Think about how you can change.

67–90: You're giving your dark side quite a free reign. Maybe you need to think about the frustrations in your life and what you can do about them. Find constructive ways of releasing aggressive energy such as working out at a gym. Do you have behaviour patterns that interfere with your career and personal relationships? Maybe it's time to change them.

54–66: You are a normal person, but you would benefit from thinking more about the sort of person you want to be. Do you really admire yourself? And are there things you do that you couldn't admit to even your closest friend?

31–53: You are an open and honest person who takes responsibility for your actions. Congratulations, you've obviously done some work on your dark side.

Under 31: You're either a saint or you're deceiving yourself. You may be a saint, but if you suspect that you're not, remember that it's important to admit to a dark side, otherwise it can unconsciously control your life. Read this book again.

Bibliography

Adler, A (1958) *Individual Psychology of Alfred Adler: A Systematic Presentation in Selections from His Writings.* HarperCollins, NY.

Assagioli, R (1974 ed) *The Act of Will.* Turnstone Press, Wellingborough, UK.

Auden, WH and Taylor, PB (1983 ed) *Norse Poems.* Faber and Faber, London.

Crowley, V (1999) *Carl Jung: Journey of Transformation — An Illustrated Biography.* Godsfield/David & Charles, Newton Abbot, UK, and (2000) Quest, Wheaton, Il.

Crowley, V (1998) *Principles of Jungian Spirituality.* Thorsons, London.

Ellenberger, HF (1970) *The Discovery of the Unconscious: The History and Evolution of Dynamic Psychiatry.* Basic Books, NY.

Ford, D (1999) *The Dark Side of the Light Chasers: Reclaiming Your Power, Creativity, Brilliance, and Dreams.* Riverhead Books, NY.

Frankl, VE (1984 ed) *Man's Search for Meaning: An introduction to logotherapy.* Touchstone, London.

Goffman, E (1990 ed) *The Presentation of Self in Everyday Life.* Penguin, NY and London.

Jung CG (1966 ed) *The Collected Works of C.G. Jung,* Volume 5, *Symbols of Transformation.* Routledge & Kegan Paul, London.

Jung CG (1966 ed) *The Collected Works of C.G. Jung,* Volume 7, *Two Essays on Analytical Psychology.* Routledge & Kegan Paul, London.

Jung CG (1966 ed) *The Collected Works of C.G. Jung,* Volume 8, *The Structure and Dynamics of the Psyche.* Routledge & Kegan Paul, London.

Jung CG (1968 ed) *The Collected Works of C.G. Jung,* Volume 9, Part 1, *Archetypes and the Collective Unconscious.* Routledge & Kegan Paul, London.

Jung CG (1968 ed) *The Collected Works of C.G. Jung,* Volume 10, *Civilization in Transition.* Routledge & Kegan Paul, London.

Jung CG (1968 ed) *The Collected Works of C.G. Jung,* Volume 11, *Psychology and Religion: West and East.* Routledge & Kegan Paul, London.

Jung CG (1970 ed) *The Collected Works of C.G. Jung,* Volume 12, *Psychology and Alchemy.* Routledge & Kegan Paul, London.

Jung CG (1966 ed) *The Collected Works of C.G. Jung,* Volume 16, *The Practice of Psychotherapy.* Routledge & Kegan Paul, London.

Kalupahana, DJ (1987) *The Principles of Buddhist Psychology.* State University of New York Press, NY.

Le Guin, UK (1979 ed) *The Earthsea Trilogy.* Penguin, Harmondsworth.

McCormick, EW (1996 ed) *Change for the Better.* Continuum, London.

Rinpoche, S (1998) *The Tibetan Book of Living and Dying.* Rider, London.

Stevenson, RL (1994 ed) *Dr Jekyll and Mr Hyde.* Penguin, NY and London.

Titchenell, EB (1985) *The Masks of Odin: Wisdom of the Ancient Norse.* Theosophical University Press, Pasadena, Ca.

Wilhelm, R (1968 ed) *I Ching or Book of Changes.* Cary F Baynes, trans, Routledge & Kegan Paul, London.

Worchel, S (1999) *Social Psychology.* Thomson Learning, Andover.